ADVANCE PRAISE

"In the world of youth development, Lou is one of few people who has broad-ranging practical expertise and experience, as well as a grounding in evidence-based approaches. I am delighted to read this book and learn from his experiences working with young people and their mentors from across the globe."

—KIRK FRIEDRICH, SENIOR CONSULTANT OF GROUNDSWELL EDUCATION AND COFOUNDER OF GRASSROOT SOCCER

"I can't think of a better person to write on the impact of relationships on young people. Lou's approach to working with child- and youth-serving agencies is an embodiment of all that he believes about the power of positive relationships."

—DENISE SILVERSTONE, DIRECTOR OF NATIONAL PROGRAMS AT THE BOYS AND GIRLS CLUBS OF CANADA

"While the power of relationships may be well understood, for years and across the globe, Lou has been powerfully breaking it down through tools, examples, and captivating stories showing that we can and must prioritize healthy relationship development with our young people to strengthen them, our communities, and our world."

—DAVID SHAPIRO, CEO, MENTOR: THE NATIONAL MENTORING PARTNERSHIP

"Lou's work serves as a compass for adults to navigate their way toward deeper, more meaningful connections with young people. When Lou charts a course for adults to connect with the young people in their lives, I follow!"

—MATT STRENG, SENIOR ADVISOR FOR YOUTH
DEVELOPMENT AT MERCY CORPS

"If you've ever wanted to pull back the curtain on what creates consistent measurable impact in the lives of children and youth, look no further. Lou's work provides a definitive roadmap to achieving it."

—LEE PAIVA, FOUNDER AND CEO OF NO MEANS NO WORLDWIDE

"Lou Bergholz is a pioneer in the designing of innovative programs that facilitate positive relationships with youth impacted by trauma, violence, poverty, and other adverse childhood experiences. He truly understands the complexity of the work with this challenging population, and he has been an inspiration to those of us in the field."

—MIA DEMARCO, CHIEF OPERATING OFFICER
OF THE JUSTICE RESOURCE INSTITUTE

"Lou Bergholz is equal parts energizing and empowering. He leads a pragmatic path into the terrain of work with challenging youth, using his deep wisdom, endless enthusiasm, and honest care to clear away obstacles and foster connections. Reading his book is the perfect antidote to the burnout experienced by those of us trying to do good."

—WENDY D'ANDREA, TRAUMA RESEARCHER AND EXPERT
AND ASSISTANT PROFESSOR AT THE NEW SCHOOL

"Our connection with Lou was vital! After the Sandy Hook tragedy, we needed help with trauma-sensitive training for our summer camp programs. Lou's experience and expertise was the perfect fit for our needs here in Newtown, and we have been using these vital tools within all of our programing to help grow beyond recovery and into a stronger and healthier community."

—AMY MANGOLD, DIRECTOR OF NEWTOWN PARKS AND RECREATION

"Lou is a curious and playful challenger of all our assumptions and taken-for-granted ways of creating social impact. His experience, creativity, and commitment to authentic pursuit of solutions spark all of us in the industry to raise our game."

—SARAH MURRAY, US DIRECTOR OF WOMEN WIN AND INTERNATIONAL SPORT AND GENDER EXECUTIVE

"Lou's work on Vital Connections takes something that seems intangible and breaks it down into skills that can be taught and practiced, making transformative youth work accessible to anyone and everyone from the volunteer sports coach to the lifelong practitioner."

—JENNIFER CLAMMER, CHIEF OF STUDENT SUPPORTS AT PHOENIX CHARTER ACADEMY NETWORK

VITAL CONNECTIONS

VITAL CONNECTIONS

Harnessing the Power of Relationship
to Impact the Lives of Young People

. . . .

LOU BERGHOLZ

LIONCREST
PUBLISHING

VITAL CONNECTIONS

*Harnessing the Power of Relationship to
Impact the Lives of Young People*

ISBN   978-1-5445-1052-1 *Paperback*

978-1-5445-1051-4 *Ebook*

For my wife, Ariana. It was working with you in Ethiopia that I was first humbled by your skill in connecting with children, and it was the very first reason I fell for you. You are my Vital Connection.

For everyone who has made the extra effort to learn a young person's name when you could have easily said, "Hey, you," who has stuck around to listen when you could have left, and who has put yourself on the line for a young person knowing you may be all they had in that moment. You know in your heart that to work with young people is to love them. This book is for you.

CONTENTS

. . . .

FOREWORD

By Judy Ross-Bernstein

* * * * * * *

I write this from Ithaca, New York, just as the leaves turn color and float downward from nearby trees. The air is newly crisp and college students seem to be everywhere, creating a sea of baseball caps and backpacks. It harkens me back to where I can easily place myself, the fall of 1992, greeting forty-five human development students on their first day of class. Their eager faces show a predictable mix of expressions, somewhere between smirk, surprise, and smile, when I initiate the conversation about our topic at hand. I pose the question, "Can you believe there is a real *course* about *children's play* at Cornell University?" (After all, play is not a serious subject worthy of study like micro-biology, is it?) In that skeptical audience sat the young Lou Bergholz, clearly an athlete, sculpted and energetic, the restlessness just a small window into his growing sense of urgency and emerging professional identity.

Lou quickly defined himself as both sharply curious and forward-moving. Over a two-year period, I saw Lou through three experiential child study courses in which the mechanisms of field placements and journal writing solidified the trust and intimacy within our mentoring relationship. Lou became an astute observer of young children, adeptly able to examine the connections between adult teaching moves and powerful developmental benefits embedded in children's play experience—belonging, self-efficacy, collaboration, creativity, and problem solving. It was through these earliest guided experiences that Lou discovered similar inextricably linked benefits to play, sport, and youth.

Delving into the potential positive outcomes, Lou was as compelled to examine negative consequences of substandard adult-child interactions and failed attempts at responsiveness. Intractable circumstances of children surfaced as well—poverty, family violence, and trauma—fueling his passion for children with challenging behaviors and marginalized populations. Lou was unafraid to ask very hard questions and to sit with harsh answers regarding systems of oppression, quality of relationships, the rights of children, and the genuine need to hear their voices. I was close enough to witness Lou's early learning toward concern for children's well-being as social justice. For Lou, children's play was a very serious subject, an authentic fit with the scholar-athlete dimensions of his emerging professional identity. Only now can I clearly see the budding activist, asking to delineate his own responsibility, who will I be in the lives of children?

Through *Vital Connections*, Lou honors the warp and weave of his intellectual spirit. We know from substantive research in human development that strong relationships matter. Urie Bronfenbrenner wisely said, "In order to develop normally, a child requires progressively more complex joint activity with one or more adults who have an irrational emotional relationship with the child." In plain speak, Bronfenbrenner continues, "Somebody's got to be crazy about that kid. That's number one. First, last, and always." I have seen Betsy McAlister Groves, director at Boston's Child Witness to Violence Project, echo the sentiment and begin a workshop by holding up one finger while saying assuredly, "This is what it takes." Yes, for all children, but especially for traumatized children, those who witness violence, that one person is unequivocally essential. Lou sees the one relationship as profound and simple: the presence of a caring adult in the life of a young person is the most important protective factor.

It is my honor to introduce Lou and his work, the culmination of risk, heart, and wisdom. *Vital Connections* has great potential to add to the expanding conversation of *how* to work with children at risk where high-quality relationships are central. That Lou deeply understands the *why* is revealed through the lived experience of his career trajectory—from positive team building with corporate executives, to developing trauma-informed relationships through play with youth worldwide. Readers will not find a cookbook approach. Instead, principles of interaction are applied to (as Bronfenbrenner put it, "joint activity") sport and play, so that the caregivers can uniquely shape their connections to their children in context. Lou addresses *how* to "be crazy about that kid." In doing so, he teaches us intentionality, professionalizing interactions that aim at belonging, self-efficacy, collaboration, creativity, and problem solving—essentially supporting resilience in children. Lou has done his homework and has the trench appeal to position himself and his work for thought leaders and practitioners hoping to make a difference in the lives of children who need them the most.

JUDY ROSS-BERNSTEIN, CHILD DEVELOPMENT CONSULTANT
AND FORMER SENIOR LECTURER IN THE DEPARTMENT OF
HUMAN DEVELOPMENT, CORNELL UNIVERSITY
ITHACA, NEW YORK
FALL 2017

Author's note: When describing the work of adults in this book, I've used their real names. These are friends, colleagues, or experts whose work I wish to acknowledge and credit. When describing young people, I've changed the names to protect their identities.

INTRODUCTION

A Missing Piece

* * * * * * *

Thailand, summer 2004. I was up early as usual; it was impossible to sleep late with the sound of ten thousand frogs croaking only a quarter mile away from our camp. We were situated in the King's Forest, north of Chiang Mai, in what appeared to be an old military barracks. A huge dirt field, which I imagine once served as a training ground for Thai soldiers, was our play space.

The main building was a long two-story cement block structure. The ground floor contained meeting rooms and an outdoor eating area. The first floor held two large rooms that functioned as sleeping quarters, accessed by narrow stairways at the ends of the building. Each side was identical: a narrow room, perhaps a hundred feet long, with small high windows. Along the walls of these bedrooms was an elevated plywood platform. I pictured the soldiers sleeping side by side in a long row, pressed tightly together like sardines in a can. Each room was large enough to sleep about fifty soldiers.

I was in Thailand with a colleague, Jules Porter. We were contracted to help design and implement a summer camp program for Thai children and adolescents infected with HIV. Many were orphans who had lost their parents to AIDS. Our task was to infuse this program with best practices from the work Jules and I had done previously with children affected by life-threatening illnesses.

Each morning at breakfast, I watched a group of excited but sleepy Thai campers eating bowls of rice and broth and pondered what we could offer to the day's programming. The Thai members of the staff had run successful camps before. They were skilled and energetic. For Jules and me, the task was to offer our ideas and experiences to make the camp even better. It was no easy assignment.

One of our primary challenges was that neither of us spoke Thai. On previous projects, we'd overcome language barriers by working with interpreters, enlisting their help to understand the many conversations that made up the pulse of the camp. Then, with the interpreter's help, we inserted ourselves into conversations and activities. Despite the inevitable time lag in conversations created by this process, it worked well.

In Thailand, our interpreter wasn't fluent in English. Nor did he fully comprehend some of the ways we were approaching youth development. This left Jules and I acutely aware of our limited capacity to engage with staff and campers. Nonetheless, we compensated with a lot of laughs, smiles, and enthusiastic body language. I'm always amazed at how much communication is possible without a common language, especially with children. On numerous occasions, I made genuine connections with the campers and staff despite not understanding what they were saying.

The most challenging part of each day came after nightfall. After evening activities, the campers marched up the stairs to their sleeping quarters. Twenty-five girls slept at one end of the barracks and twenty-five boys slept at the other, on thin mattresses, each with a single blanket. Like the soldiers who used the barracks before them, they slept in tight formation.

Once the campers were upstairs, we pulled a few benches together downstairs to plan the next day's agenda. Even without translation, Jules and I understood that the staff were investing a tremendous amount of time and energy into planning. They were absolutely committed to programming the next day in remarkable detail, from logistics, to roles, to activities.

These meetings stretched well over an hour, sometimes

two. Even with an interpreter, Jules and I found it difficult to keep up with the conversations, which made it challenging to interject with ideas or suggestions. We resigned ourselves to taking a back seat.

Freed from the minutiae of logistics, however, I was struck by the feeling that we were missing a crucial opportunity. Above us lay fifty children. They were far from home, lying in an unfamiliar bedroom. The room itself was pitch dark and uncomfortably hot, even for children accustomed to Thai weather. During the night, the thousands of frogs living so close to the camp made a tremendous noise, which I imagined some of the children must have found frightening.

As I listened to the approximately fifteen members of staff, all dedicated to giving these young campers the best week of their young lives, I felt that something *was* missing. The schedule for the following day was crucial, but so was the experience of the campers in that moment. Why wasn't anyone upstairs with them, tucking them in?

Although these thoughts occurred to me, I didn't want to interrupt their meeting, and my job was to support the staff. I felt obliged to stay in the meetings and contribute what I could. That is, until Karn stepped in. Karn, one of the younger members of staff, was from Norway. She had lived in Thailand for several years and spoke the language well. She stood up and quietly walked up the stairs to the girls' sleeping room. Jules and I, curious about what she was doing, decided to follow her.

At the top of the stairs, Karn quietly opened the door and slipped in. When we peeked through the door, she was already sitting on the edge of the plywood bed, leaning over one of the girls. Despite the heat, almost every girl was wrapped tightly in their blanket, a telltale sign that they were in need of a little comfort. Karn sat and whispered with the first girl for maybe a minute, and then she moved on to the next. I was mesmerized. She repeated this with each of the girls, before standing up and walking outside. She hadn't realized we were observing her, so she was surprised to see us standing there. Unable to contain our curiosity, we asked Karn what she had done.

"I wanted to do for each girl what my mother used to do for me when I went to bed," she explained. "I sit with each of them and tell them, 'Even though it's dark out, and you're tired, and you might feel alone, you're not. I'm here with you. Sometimes the hardest part is falling asleep. And the best thing is that once you fall asleep, you get to dream. A dream can take you wherever you want. So I need to wrap you up like a package so we can be sure you get where you want to go.'

"I tuck them in tight. I push the blanket under them on

both sides. I make sure the blanket is tucked in under their chin. Then I say, 'Now that you're all bundled up, you have to decide where you want to go. Remember, it's a dream, so you can choose. Do you want to go back to your school, visit your parents, go home, play with your friends, do an activity you did today at camp?'

"Wherever they want to go, I ask for specifics. I need those details so I can address the package. 'You can't travel anywhere without an address,' I tell them. Then I write what they tell me gently on their chest with my finger. 'OK,' I say, 'you're wrapped up and ready to go. You have your address. But you can't travel without stamps. We need stamps! How many stamps do you need?' They might say 'three' or 'four.' If they know what's coming next, they might say 'ten' or 'twelve.' For each stamp they request, I give them a gentle kiss on the forehead.

"Finally, I say to each girl, 'OK, you're all wrapped up. You have your address. You have your stamps. Now you can close your eyes and you get to travel in your dreams where you want to go. When you wake up, I'll be here and we'll have a great day at camp. Safe travels and sweet dreams.'"

Whenever I facilitate workshops or engage in conversations about working with young people, I find myself coming back to this story. It was a brief interaction, but it had a major impact on me and marked a definitive shift in my approach to working with young people. So much of what you will read here has its genesis in what I witnessed Karn doing intuitively with these girls at bedtime. By acknowledging that the children at that camp were struggling with difficult emotions and giving them one small tool to deal with those emotions, she also opened a door for me.

A QUEST FOR ANSWERS

For much of my direct service work with young people, I was primarily an activities guy. I've spent a large portion of my career writing curricula and designing interventions for youth programs around the world. In my early twenties, my nickname around camp was Rolodex because I carried hundreds of index cards with the names of games written on them, ready to pull one out and play at any moment. That all started to change in 1998 when I began working with a population of young people affected by illness.

At the beginning of that year, I was living in Cleveland. By March, I had packed up my car and moved to a small town in northeastern Connecticut, the home of the Hole in the Wall Gang Camp. This camp, founded a decade earlier, was the brainchild of Paul Newman. It was dedicated to a single, unique purpose: providing children in the northeastern United States who were living with illnesses such as cancer, sickle cell anemia, hemophilia, or HIV with an opportunity to attend summer camp. It was their chance to do all the "normal" activities that healthy children do without a second thought: swimming, theater, cookouts, and in Newman's words, "raising a little hell."

I was hired as the adventure director, responsible for the programming on a low- and high-ropes course. With a staff of two, I worked each week to use elements built into the trees to create the best possible adventure for cabins of campers. Naturally, I threw myself into the work, applying everything I thought I knew about great youth development. Much like the camp staff in Thailand, my staff and I worked late at night and rose early in the morning. We sequenced activities to maximize learning, created story lines and characters, dressed up in costume, and once even built a giant cardboard *Star Wars* monster called Pizza the Hut who, when fed plastic gold coins (earned from participating in activities), proceeded to spit out popsicles. My "activities guy" persona was firing on all cylinders.

Each afternoon, my staff and I worked with a cabin of eight campers at our adventure tower. The campers wore a harness, clipped into a safety line, and attempted to climb a thirty-foot wooden tower. It was an intense and moving experience. These young people were already confronting their own mortality, at a far younger age than anyone should. In addition, they were putting their lives in the hands of their peers and staff. Their courage inspired in me a sense of humility and appreciation for life and death that I hadn't previously experienced.

At the end of each tower session, our team of three began the time-consuming process of packing up the equipment and securing the tower for the night. As the summer progressed, I found myself at a philosophical impasse with one of my team members, Jenny. She insisted on leaving during cleanup, walking to dinner with the campers, and sharing a meal with them. At the time, it made no sense to me. The children had cabin counselors. Our job was to give them activities. Just like Karn, Jenny sometimes visited the children's cabin in the evening and sat with them while they got ready for bed. Again, I didn't understand her motivation. In my mind, that time was crucial for planning the next day's activities. Why would she give that up to sit with campers while they brushed their teeth or lay in bed falling asleep?

Since that experience in Connecticut, I have been on a journey that is still ongoing today—a journey that has led me to look at the needs of young people in a different way and shift my approach from a focus on activities to a focus on what I call Vital Connections. Looking back, my early youth work experiences played a major role in planting the seeds of what would eventually become the topic of this book: recognizing, accessing, and utilizing those Vital Connections.

I've always loved working with young people. From teaching swim lessons in Pittsburgh in the mid-eighties to working as a camp counselor in the early nineties, I kept coming back to roles that gave me the opportunity to try to make a difference in the lives of children and adolescents. It wasn't until the early 2000s, however, that I fully understood the direction my career would take.

After studying human development and family studies at Cornell between 1990 and 1994, I departed for Israel, where part of my work involved creating an ad hoc after-school program, primarily for Ethiopian and Yugoslavian children. Returning to the United States, I taught human sexuality to middle and high schoolers in Maine, then relocated to New Mexico to work at a residential facility in the Santa Fe National Forest for adolescents with severe learning disabilities and behavioral challenges. I ran the gym at a Boys and Girls Club in Cleveland. And, as described above, I facilitated an adventure program at a summer camp for children and adolescents with life-threatening illnesses.

Although I was unaware of it at the time, my journey was slowly developing an intense focus, as I became preoccupied with the question of how to achieve the strongest possible outcomes with limited programmatic resources. Toward the end of summer 1998, I settled in Boston. A few years after that, I founded Edgework, the consulting firm that has now become the vehicle through which I and the rest of our team work, with a broad range of clients, on interpersonal, team, and organizational projects. These formative youth development experiences became the building blocks of Edgework—and our relationship-centric approach.

Almost all the stories in this book occurred between 1994 and 2008. Looking back on that fifteen-year period, I recognize two pivotal insights that have since played a central role in shaping my overall philosophy about youth work. First, context is everything. By context, I mean everything that a young person experiences outside the specific program they are engaged in. Context includes culture, community, and the relationships they have with family, friends, and others. It includes all the major social and economic influences in their lives, along with the setting they call home. Context is ever-present. It is a crucial and sacred element of working with young people and one that I attend to closely whenever I think about creating an intervention.

The second insight is that there are some aspects of working with young people that are nearly universal. I can't say that a specific technique or approach will work in every single situation. Undoubtedly, they must be adapted to different cultures and contexts. Yet there are some basic principles that are remarkably consistent. As I spent time with skilled youth workers from Ithaca to Malawi to Gaza, I was consistently struck by how certain ways of engaging with young people seemed to transcend language and culture, and how so much of what children and adolescents need, at the most basic level, is love.

THE POWER OF VITAL CONNECTIONS

I was scheduled to return to northern Thailand in summer 2005 to manage another round of camps. On December 26, 2004, an earthquake in the Indian Ocean caused a series of tsunamis that struck southern Thailand and many other parts of Southeast Asia. Conservative estimates state that approximately 230,000 people, in fourteen countries, lost their lives as a direct result of the disaster. In Thailand, more than five thousand people were killed and another sixteen thousand were injured, displaced, or reported missing.

In the aftermath of the tsunami, the needs of young people in the south of the country changed radically. Thousands of children and adolescents were displaced. Some had lost family members. Many were exhibiting signs of trauma.

I returned to Thailand as planned, but not for camp work. I was now working closely with another skilled youth development professional, Aly Fox. As part of our ongoing work with the SeriousFun Network, we had developed a set of child-centered games and techniques, which were used with programs working with young people affected by illness and other vulnerabilities. We were asked to bring some of this work to several youth development organizations in parts of Thailand badly affected by the tsunami. Our role was to work with program staff, providing them with additional knowledge and practical tools that they could use in service of the young people in their communities.

As we learned about the existing support mechanisms and resources in these communities, I pondered the best ways to be useful for this population of staff. I kept thinking about what I had experienced back at the adventure tower in 1998 and during my camp work the previous year in Thailand. I thought about Jenny, who opted to spend evenings sitting with campers over dinner. I thought back a year earlier to Karn's kindness as she helped each girl in that former military barracks fall asleep. The more I reflected, the more I realized that there was something protective, even strengthening, that occurred when adults engaged with young people in just the right way. Yet the impact didn't necessarily come from activities or lesson plans. This was a radical reversal of my approach to that point, yet the more I explored it, the more I found it both exciting and confusing.

I come from a long line of bookworms in my family, each

of us with well-stocked libraries filling every corner of our homes, so I turned to something I have always relied on to make sense of the complexities of the world: research. I started by reading the work of leading child development and attachment theorists such as John Bowlby, Mary Ainsworth, Albert Bandura, and Urie Bronfenbrenner. Soon, I was deeply immersed in the study of resilience, exploring the work of Martha Bragin, James Anthony, Bertram Cohler, Martin Seligman, Junlei Li, Megan Julian, Sam Goldstein, Robert Brooks, Bonnie Benard, and many others.

I knew I was heading to Thailand to try to support staff who were working with young people struggling with tremendous risk factors such as displacement and loss of loved ones. Time and resources were limited. I wanted to know the answer to one crucial question: What has the greatest impact on a young person's life?

The answer I discovered was simple and profound. Everything I read pointed to the presence of a caring adult as the most important protective factor in the life of a young person. There are many other relevant factors, including high self-efficacy, self-awareness, school attendance, positive peer relationships, and opportunities to belong. Overwhelmingly, however, research suggested that a relationship with a caring adult is primary.

John Bowlby and Mary Ainsworth first developed attachment theory in the 1950s. In 1979, developmental psychologist Urie Bronfenbrenner wrote, "No society can long sustain itself unless its members have learned the sensitivities, motivations, and skills involved in assisting and caring for other human beings."[1]

James Anthony and Bertram Cohler, in their book on resilience, *The Invulnerable Child*, concluded that the secure relationship between a caring adult and a child was the most important protective factor.[2] In 2015, the National Scientific Counsel on the Developing Child concluded:

Whether the burdens come from hardships of poverty, the challenges of parental substance abuse or serious mental illness, the stresses of war, the threats of recurrent violence or chronic neglect, or a combination of factors, the single most common finding is that children who end up doing well have had at least one stable and committed relationship with a supportive parent, caregiver, or other adult.[3]

---

1   Urie Bronfenbrenner, *The Ecology of Human Development* (Cambridge, MA: Harvard University Press, 1979).

2   E. James Anthony and Bertram J. Cohler, *The Invulnerable Child* (New York: Guilford, 1987).

3   National Scientific Council on the Developing Child, "Supportive Relationships and Active Skill-Building Strengthen the Foundations of Resilience" (working paper 13, Center on the Developing Child, Harvard University, Cambridge, MA, 2015), www.developingchild.edu.

When I first absorbed this research, I experienced it as a jolt to my mental model about youth development. Much of my career was built on investing a huge amount of time into activities creation, curriculum design, and intentional programming. The research was so compelling, however, that it stopped me in my tracks. While I was learning games and trying to write complex curricula, should I have been doing something else? I would come to realize that great programming is important, but not as important as I had imagined.

I wanted to learn everything I could about how to be the caring adult I had read about. Intuitively, I understood the concept. Yet I also wanted more. I knew that I couldn't stand in front of a group of youth workers and simply tell them to care for the young people they work with. What I needed was the *how*.

As I expanded my research, I began to look for the answer to this question. I read more articles and books, searching for techniques, strategies, and even phrases that a caring adult could use to make the most of every interaction with a young person. It soon became apparent that while the fundamental value of the caring adult was well documented, learning how to be that caring adult was far less straightforward. I broadened my inquiries, quizzing experts and skilled youth workers in hopes of teasing out their most valuable insights.

Before I left for Thailand in summer 2005, I had identified four distinct skills and collectively named them Vital Connections. They formed a significant portion of the multiday training we delivered.

On the first day of the training, we asked each participant to share stories about caring adults who made a significant difference to their lives when they were young. It was moving and meaningful to hear so many people describe how they were shaped by these Vital Connections. By the time the workshops concluded, I knew I was hooked on this topic and that I was on a continuing quest to understand exactly how these Vital Connections work in the lives of young people. At the time, I didn't realize that they'd become the fulcrum of my work for the next decade and beyond.

The more I understood about Vital Connections, the more meaningful I found Karn's delicate intervention in the camp in northern Thailand. In the light of that story, many of the concepts and ideas I was tinkering with in my evolving approach to working with young people crystallized and took shape. For example:

- There is so much more going on for a young person than we can see. Their inner world is complex and intense and not always easy to access.
- Often, even the most well-intentioned and well-

designed activities do not work the same way for every young person. Sometimes they don't work at all.

- Timing is everything. I may be scheduled to work at a certain time, but this doesn't necessarily correlate with the times at which young people are able to show up, participate, and absorb the lessons I have planned.
- Not all interactions have the same impact. Some things I say or do seem to penetrate much deeper than I anticipate, while others are nowhere near as effective as I expect them to be.
- Love is more powerful than I ever imagined.
- Lying in a strange bed at night, far away from home, is one of the loneliest moments anyone can experience, no matter how old they are.

THE SIX VITAL CONNECTIONS

Since 2005, through ongoing research, design, and practice, I have expanded the original four Vital Connections to six. Simultaneously, many other researchers and organizations have dedicated themselves to studying the role of caring adults in the lives of young people. Our understanding of the importance of caring adults has deepened, and this topic has entered the mainstream. Schools, afterschool programs, camps, coaches, teachers, caregivers, and many other practitioners are applying principles from research about the value of caring adults to their interactions with children and adolescents.

Personally, I like to have the "what," but I also very much need the "how." This book has been written to provide you with a healthy dose of both the "what" and the "how." Perhaps you work with young people in a professional capacity or are researching some aspect of youth development. Perhaps you're a parent, a grandparent, or even a friend to a young person. My hope is that you will feel validated by these six Vital Connections. You should be able to finish a chapter, put down the book, and use something you read immediately with a young person in your life. Here are the six Vital Connections I'll be exploring in this book.

MAKE TIME AT THE RIGHT TIME

The lives of some young people are scheduled and programmed from the time they wake up until they go to sleep. Others may spend large blocks of time on their own: after school, in the evening, or even overnight. In both cases, the time these young people spend interacting meaningfully with the adults in their lives may be counted in minutes, not hours. There are many times when they need the support and guidance of caring adults, yet schedules may not align. To reach them, you need to be there when they need you, not just when you have the time. Your ability to have a positive impact on their lives stems from being there at the right times for *them*.

KNOW THEIR STORY

It never ceases to amaze and sadden me how many people in the world, both children and adults, feel isolated and alone, believing that nobody understands or cares about them. To be known is to feel a sense of belonging. To be unknown is to feel lost and often hopeless. It is this act of getting to know someone that allows a relationship to form. If you want to help young people, you must find ways to get to know their story. When you do this, you increase your commitment to them. Often, this increases their commitment to you as well. Knowing who they are maximizes the chances that you will be able to work with them in a way that will be of real benefit.

BELIEVE THEY CAN SUCCEED

We all carry around a story we tell about ourselves. These narratives shape our self-esteem and our sense of self-efficacy. They contain our ideas of what we believe we can achieve. Research on child development indicates that we develop our self-assessments at an early age and that these assessments are heavily influenced by what key adults in our lives say about us. As an adult, this gives you a tremendous opportunity to have a positive impact on the stories the young people in your care tell themselves. You can promote and advocate your belief that they can succeed and encourage them to take ownership of that belief.

SUPPORT VITAL CONVERSATIONS

There are times when a conversation can influence a decision, help us gain important insights into ourselves, and even reshape our lives. Even young children need to engage in this type of meaningful dialogue with adults. These are vital conversations. When you know how to recognize and anticipate vital conversations, you can make yourself available for these special moments, potentially with major positive impact. It's true that the name of this Vital Connection sounds very similar to the overall title of this book, and yet I've found no better way to describe it than with the word *vital*. It is simply vital that young people have the chance to engage in deep, focused conversations with caring adults.

FACILITATE CONNECTIONS WITH OTHER CARING ADULTS

No adult—not even a parent—can be all things to a young person. Helping children and teenagers forge relationships with other caring adults can be a powerful form of support. Sometimes other people can provide something that you can't or are available when you're not. In those instances, the greatest service you can offer may be to broaden the network of caring adults available to a young person.

INTERVENE WHEN THEY NEED YOU MOST

There may be times when a young person in your care

has a need that stretches beyond what you were hired to provide, yet you feel compelled to help. A timely intervention could prevent a tragedy or create an opportunity that would otherwise never have existed for a young person in need. This final Vital Connection is unlike the other five. It may test your professional boundaries. Yet there may be times when a young person has a need that you are able to meet and—despite the challenges or risks—you choose to intervene *because* of the commitment you have for that young person.

HARNESSING THE POWER OF RELATIONSHIP

Karn's transformation of a lonely, scary moment for those twenty-five girls in northern Thailand set me on a mission to discover how to harness the power of relationship to have the greatest possible impact on the lives of young people. To this day, I consider it one of the best individual moments of youth work I have ever witnessed. She embodied the caring adult, supporting those girls as they faced their fears and helping them to tap into their own reservoir of strength and security. Karn's compassionate approach fostered each girl's sense of agency, as she met them where and when they needed her the most and became a gentle light in their darkness.

My interest in studying the role of caring adults in the lives of young people has lasted more than a decade and continues to unfold. Even as I write this book, I'm actively searching for any and all things that can contribute to this endeavor. As you read this book, I invite you to do the same. The Vital Connections described in this book are intended, first and foremost, to be the foundation of a mindset, not simply information to be passively consumed. This mindset is based on the premise that relationships can transform. Intentional activities, strong program culture, and positive peer relationships all play important roles in shaping young people's lives, but Vital Connections matter more.

Each Vital Connection may challenge some of your assumptions and practices. You will be invited to extend the time you spend with young people, get closer to their story, engage in deeper and more difficult conversations, and invest more in them. Many of you are already stretched thin with your time and feel exhausted by the demands of your roles and responsibilities. I know that contemplating giving even more can seem overwhelming. Burnout in direct service youth work is a real concern. As you read about each Vital Connection, therefore, look for what you can handle. It's my hope that you will find techniques and approaches in these pages that—far from costing you precious time and energy—can save you time, increase your energy and commitment to the work, and amplify your impact.

The order of the six Vital Connections is intentional. As

you work through each one, think about how they build on each other. The sequencing of the Vital Connections helps us develop the skill and capacity to leverage our power as caring adults. The first two, **Make Time at the Right Time** and **Know Their Story**, are the basics. They are about time and attention. They challenge you to show up and take a genuine interest in the young people you are working with.

The middle two, **Believe They Can Succeed** and **Support Vital Conversations**, are more sophisticated. They require deeper levels of interaction and will test your belief in the young people in your care. They will ask you to take conversations where young people need them to go, not just where you feel comfortable. To succeed in applying these two Vital Connections, you will need to truly care about the young people you work with.

The final two, **Facilitate Connections with Other Caring Adults** and **Intervene When They Need You Most**, tend to arise after you've formed a genuine relationship with a specific young person. They remind us that it "takes a village to raise a child" and that the most powerful Vital Connection sometimes involves an action based primarily on commitment and love.

Nonetheless, it would be a mistake to assume that the Vital Connections always flow neatly in order and that you can move from one to the other in a predetermined pattern. Young people will need your support in different ways at different times, and it would be impossible to write a book that covered all eventualities. Please feel free to make use of them at the right times, in the right ways, for the young people you care about.

As you read this book, you may notice that the chapters vary in length. Chapters three and four, for example, are far longer than chapters one and two. This reflects the fact that Vital Connections operate in the real world and don't always fit neatly into boxes. Put simply, in the journey to uncover how caring adults have the most impact possible, I have found more to say about some Vital Connections than others. However, don't assume that a certain Vital Connection is more important than another by the length of its chapter. Each Vital Connection possesses its own powerful potential to be just what a certain young person needs from you.

Each young person you work with is a unique, complicated, wonderful, and, at times, frustrating individual. They need you, even though they may not tell you this very often—or sometimes ever. After all the research I've done and the experiences I've had working with young people, what makes this book on Vital Connections so special to me is that I believe it offers a way inside the world of the young people you care about.

Vital Connections are not simply about research. They are about hearing the voices of young people. They are about tuning into their needs and hearing them when they say, "Sit with me. Listen to me. Know me. Believe in me. Be there for me when I need you most."

Before you turn the page, think about the young people in your life at this moment. Read this book with one or two, or ten, of them in mind. As you learn about each of the six Vital Connections, keep those young people in your thoughts. If you listen closely, I hope you will hear their voices echoing through these pages.

PART ONE

· · · · · · ·

TIME AND STORY

CHAPTER ONE

MAKE TIME AT THE RIGHT TIME

* * * * * * *

Kirk Friedrich and I met in high school, during preseason tryouts for the soccer team. We were both newcomers, having moved that summer from Massachusetts and Pennsylvania, respectively. Kirk was a freshman, I a senior, and both of us would go on to play college soccer. After college, Kirk traveled to play professionally in the Zimbabwean Premier League. He and some of his teammates were deeply affected by the HIV crisis, which was at its peak while he was playing in the country. Southern Africa was widely impacted by HIV, and in Zimbabwe at the time it was estimated that one in three adults were HIV-positive. Kirk and his teammates began to wonder whether professional soccer players, using the game as a "playing field" for teaching and talking about HIV, could play a role in the prevention effort. He joined forces with three of his teammates and friends—Tommy

Clark, Methembe Ndlovu, and Ethan Zohn—to launch Grassroot Soccer.

That was when he reached out to me. We had lost touch after I graduated from high school in 1990, but over a decade later, he saw an opportunity to involve me in contributing to the design of the program. On my first and only visit to Zimbabwe, Kirk and I spent most of our time holed up in a house in Bulawayo, in front of our laptops, talking through activities and writing up lessons on how soccer could play a meaningful role in HIV prevention.

Looking back on that first curriculum, I realize that there were significant gaps in our knowledge of public health, behavior change, and the complicated realities of decision making that children and adolescents face. But we knew what could engage young people, and we had a lot of ideas and energy. Early in the process, we recognized that activities alone would not be sufficient to achieve the outcomes we sought to achieve. For me, the work with Grassroot Soccer also became an important early testing ground for using concepts and practices of Vital Connections that I had been developing. Kirk and his cofounders were wonderfully open, encouraging, and willing to try some of the early iterations of Vital Connections. Through extensive piloting and evaluation, Grassroot Soccer has become a pioneering force in the field of sport for social change.

I continued working with Grassroot Soccer through 2010, as it expanded its programming into multiple countries across Africa. Kirk and his colleagues started to convene master coaches and trainers for advanced training and professional development. I was responsible for designing and delivering these events in Zambia and South Africa. One of the most important connections I made during this period was with a young woman named Sithethelelwe Sibanda, or Kwinji, to her friends.

Kwinji was the captain of the Zimbabwean women's national soccer team. She also played for a local women's semiprofessional team in Bulawayo and was one of a handful of the first players recruited by Grassroot Soccer to become coaches for the program. A natural leader, she later undertook advanced training and became a master coach.

I knew of Kwinji's reputation before we met. She was known for her ability to refer girls in her program to additional services such as HIV and pregnancy testing and for intervening where she saw neglect or abuse. By that stage of my career, I had fully embraced the idea that not all the best solutions to the challenges facing young people could be uncovered through surveys or randomized control trials. Sometimes the best solutions are found in someone's personal practice and approach to their work.

I wanted to talk to her and find out what was she doing differently. How was she, more than any of the other coaches, discovering what the girls in the Grassroot Soccer program needed? So one day I asked her what she was doing that made her so successful. "I don't know," she replied in her usual soft-spoken way.

It was a completely honest answer but also unsatisfying. I inquired again, and again she gave me a similar response. One of the techniques I've learned in my work on Vital Connections is to ask the question, "How did you do that?" You'll read about it in detail in chapter three. For now, suffice to say that it's a wonderful technique to encourage an adult or child who needs a gentle nudge to reflect on their own behavior. After asking Kwinji this question several times in succession, I began to understand the simple brilliance of her approach.

Kwinji liked to play soccer. After a session, she sometimes stayed behind to kick a ball around, purely for her own enjoyment. She enjoyed connecting with the girls in the Grassroot Soccer program, so she invited them to join her. Often, a girl would stay and kick the ball with Kwinji. This girl would then stick around again after the next session. This was a signal to Kwinji that the girl might have something on her mind. Sometimes Kwinji initiated the conversation; sometimes the girl spoke up first. Either way, Kwinji began to learn about what was going on in the girl's life. Sometimes, that would be the end of the story.

However, other times, Kwinji would uncover something more sensitive. Kwinji would then intervene to try and get the girl the help she needed. This was only possible because she knew, intuitively, how to **make time at the right time**.

Kwinji and I were thousands of miles away from the King's Forest in northern Thailand. Four years had elapsed since that camp, yet I found myself thinking about those girls lying in the dark on their plywood bed, wrapped up tightly in their blankets, waiting for their stamps. I realized there was something important threading those two stories together.

The girls in Thailand needed a counselor the most at bedtime, after a full day of activities. Similarly, some of the girls in Bulawayo needed their coach the most *after* a Grassroot Soccer session. The time they spent with Kwinji wasn't even part of the official program. It followed after the formal activities and conversations relating to sexuality, pregnancy, and HIV. What some of the girls needed could only be provided outside the program, in the informal and even safer space Kwinji had created. It was also the time when she could have the greatest impact.

The right time for a young person is when they need you. It could be during an activity. However, it might also be while setting up cones before a soccer practice or cleaning up after an art activity. It could be as you walk through the neighborhood together. Conventional wisdom about youth programs such as Grassroot Soccer's says that we should envision the outcomes we aspire to achieve happening during this program time.

Kwinji helped me to realize that this isn't necessarily the case. After speaking to her, I understood that if I wanted to help a young person with a critical need, making myself available during informal time, the time hiding in and around the formality of a program, was fundamentally important.

FOSTERING CONNECTION DURING INFORMAL TIME IN GAZA

Around the same time I was working with Kwinji and Grassroot Soccer, I was consulting to a camp for vulnerable children in Malawi, named Children in the Wilderness (CITW). By 2008, the program had garnered enough success to receive funding from the United States Agency for International Development (USAID).

The next time I traveled to Malawi, my fourth visit, I met Martha Myers, a representative of USAID who was championing the funding of our work. Martha had worked in international development for decades, including many years of experience in the Middle East. While we were in Malawi, she told me that she was planning to return to the Middle East, specifically to Jerusalem, to become the regional director of CARE's West Bank-Gaza office. Impressed by the outcomes she had observed in the camp in Malawi, Martha wondered whether some form of a camp model could work in Gaza.

Gaza is a complicated place to live. The politics and history of the region keep it regularly in the news spotlight. Rockets and bombs sail back and forth across its borders. And the effects of this instability and violence on mental health are pervasive. In 2009, a United Nations Population Fund study revealed that 100 percent of the women surveyed reported symptoms of trauma and stress, including an inability to care for their children and families.[4] A separate survey, conducted by CARE International in that same year, found that 95 percent of adult respondents reported fear and signs of distress among their children.[5] These signs included bed-wetting, nightmares, and a host of learning challenges. Unsurprisingly, the study also discovered pervasive peer-to-peer and family violence, depression, and anxiety.

Martha explained that many types of interventions had been tried in Gaza. Some had worked, but most had little

4   Culture and Free Thought Association and the United Nations Population Fund, "Gaza Crisis: Psycho-Social Consequences for Women," February 2009 (https://unispal.un.org/DPA/DPR/unispal.nsf/0/50205F1E9F475273852575680059D75A).

5   Archived press release, http://www.carewbg.org/media/preleases/pr26012009.pdf (retrieved March 20, 2012).

to no impact. She expressed an interest in trying some-thing different. She told me that one of her beliefs about working in Gaza was that people couldn't be expected to make peace with another—in this case, Israelis—if they couldn't make peace within themselves. She proposed creating an after-school program for Gazan children, built on principles of social and emotional development, and some of the core values of the camp we had developed in Malawi. It was an ambitious project. The goal was to make a measurable dent in the many-layered mental health difficulties faced by children in Gaza.

Later in 2009, Martha won the grant and contacted me to discuss designing the program. "What do you want to do?" she asked. I knew immediately. Believing in the power of caring adults as the most important protective factor for young people, I wanted to design the intervention around this vital relationship. Martha agreed to this approach, and I set about creating the program in Gaza, built on the principles of Vital Connections, named Eye to the Future (E2F). E2F gave me my first opportunity to embed Vital Connections throughout every corner of a program. It was also an opportunity to learn from the wisdom of Kwinji and incorporate her approach on a formal basis.

The program was aimed at children between nine and twelve years old, who attended three times per week for two and a half hours per day. We launched at three of the sites most heavily affected by recent bombings—Beit Lahia, Beit Hanoun, and East Gaza—and ran the program twice a day, once in the mornings and once in the afternoons. Each cohort consisted of twenty-five children. By running the program six days per week, we accommodated four cohorts per site—two morning groups and two afternoon groups—simultaneously. This meant we could serve a hundred children per site in every six-month cycle.

Working with the leadership and staff at each site, we developed many activities intended to support the outcomes of the project, such as art, singing, tutoring, theater, and more. The result was an enriching, fun, and educational program. Aware that it would take more than activities to create a Vital Connection, however, we also took a page out of Kwinji's book and thought carefully about the time before and after scheduled activities.

Morning sessions started at 9:00 a.m., but children started to arrive well before that time. This was a common phenomenon at many schools in Gaza. Hundreds of children arrived early and lined the sidewalks outside the locked school gates. They crowded around the entrances, waiting for the moment the gates were opened and they could stream inside to their first class.

The area outside our program buildings contained a small but functional playground space, so we decided to give the children access to those spaces prior to the official beginning of the program. We opened the gates half an hour early, encouraging the children to come in, put their bags down safely inside, and play outdoors. We also required all staff join the children in the playground. The rules of engagement were clear and intentional. Members of staff were not allowed to cluster together or lead any formal activities. During informal time before the program, their goal was simply to connect with the children.

At first, many members of staff were confused by this aspect of the program design. They were accustomed to a more traditional school culture and more formal interactions with children in classroom settings. To tackle their resistance, we paid them for the additional time and trained them about the importance of informal time. We talked about Vital Connections, discussed how and when relationships form, and I even told the story of Kwinji. Some were convinced, while others remained skeptical. Nonetheless, we succeeded in initiating this practice at all three sites.

The effects were nothing short of remarkable. By the time the first six-month cohort of children had completed the program, all members of staff across all three sites fully embraced this preprogram informal time. They shared story after story, telling us what they had learned about the children. They commented on the ways in which the connections they were forming with the children during these times shaped the way they worked with the children during the formal activities. Knowing more about individual children, they felt able to teach more effectively. Facilitating informal discussions on problem solving, for example, they gained a better understanding of how individual children thought and processed information and experiences. This enabled them to adapt lessons, making them more meaningful. On several occasions, it became apparent that individual children needed additional support services. One boy disclosed that he was considering suicide, and members of staff succeeded in intervening to give him the support he and his family needed.

There's no simple formula to calculate the value of the time you spend with a young person. Unfortunately, many young people find themselves bouncing off the adults in their lives, never connecting deeply. In a classroom of twenty, thirty, or even fifty classmates, the actual time each young person engages directly with caring adults can be counted in minutes, perhaps even seconds. After school, they may or may not have access to their caring adults. This makes any opportunity to connect with them even more valuable.

WHEN IS THE RIGHT TIME?

Why does making time at the right time matter so much?

All of us, children and adults, need people when *we* need them. Unfortunately, our worlds are rarely set up to allow that level of responsiveness. There's a reason why so many caregivers struggle to balance time with their children and time spent at work and managing a household. There's a reason why many teachers wonder about the students who are already in the parking lot before they arrive in the morning, waiting for school to begin. There's a reason why the coach feels a heavy sense of responsibility when she shuts down the gym at the end of the day and knows that the *next* hour may be when the teenagers she trains need her the most.

I love to hear about people and organizations that take making time at the right time to heart. One type of program in the United States that epitomizes this Vital Connection is midnight basketball. Founded in Maryland in 1986, midnight basketball creates opportunities for young adults to play basketball between approximately 10:00 p.m. and 2:00 a.m. Why those times? Because that window of time is critical for adolescents and young people. If they're not on a basketball court, they could be out without supervision, potentially making decisions that take them down a risky path. I don't know many adults who relish the idea of heading out to work at 10:00 p.m., especially on a Friday or Saturday night. To reach vulnerable young people when they are most in need, however, it's essential to be present at that time.

Most Boys and Girls Clubs operate on a similar principle. They aim to keep their doors open well into the evening, sometimes until 9:00 or 10:00 p.m., because the club directors and leadership know that many of the children and adolescents who attend may not have many other positive places during those after-school and evening hours. Between 1992 and 1997, I worked on and off at a Boys and Girls Club in Cleveland, Ohio. I regularly saw seven-year-olds who were dropped off after school at 3:00 p.m. and stayed until closing. It's a savior for caregivers working second shift or who may not be able to afford babysitters. For many of the children, the club was the safest place for them to be during that time, while also offering enrichment and engagement.

Both midnight basketball and Boys and Girls Clubs highlight how our orientation to youth work can change when we look closely at what it means to make time at the right time. For anyone working in a structured program, however, the desire to meet young people at the time *they* need can be a source of tension. Never forget that formal activities are important. They provide a reliable, consistent curriculum and a chance for us as adults to meet young people when we *think* they need us. This approach is valuable as long as we're also willing to adapt to unexpected or unstated needs.

Sometimes they may arrive early to first period class or

linger after a basketball practice. They may call or text at off-hour times. Young people know when we are making ourselves available to them, and when we're not. They draw strength and resilience from the times when we do.

Never underestimate the importance of your presence. Think about when you could surrender the organizing and facilitating of activities and simply give your time to young people who need you.

Recognize, too, that this Vital Connection applies equally to adult relationships. We also have a deep need for other caring adults to show up when we need them most. As I write this book, my wife is in the middle of a three-year pediatric residency program. She works, on average, eighty hours per week, waking up almost every day at 5:30 or 6:00 a.m. and returning home after 7:00 p.m. or later.

Most nights, she is exhausted and ready for bed by 8:30 p.m. In the summer months, this is quite comical, because it's light outside until after 9:30 p.m. Despite this, most nights we draw down the blinds and go to bed together. I am a late-night person by nature, but I've come to value this early bedtime. These are the most important minutes of our day for us to make time at the right time.

PUTTING IT INTO PRACTICE: MAKING TIME AT THE RIGHT TIME

This section offers some key ways to put the principle of making time at the right time into practice. The first is to **distinguish between formal time and informal time.** Understand that while these two types of time are both important, they are different in crucial ways.

Formal time is for planned activities. It is designed, scheduled, or activity-based. Informal time is unstructured, relaxed, or transitional. As Kwinji's story demonstrates, sometimes informal time gives young people a space in which they feel free to express their real concerns. In addition, informal time tends to facilitate relationship building. This is why, as adults, we may get to know some of our work colleagues faster by going out for dinner with them than by working with them.

There are several ways to build connections during informal time. The first is to **be "on" during informal time.** It may be an activity break for the participants, but it shouldn't be for you. You may want to assign staff to work actively during break times or recess. If you need to prepare for scheduled activities so that you're free during informal time, consider arriving early so that you can finish setting up in time to greet your participants as they arrive. Eat lunch with the young people in your care, or make the most of water or snack breaks. Think about ways to make transition times more special. There are games to play, songs to sing, and conversations to have. Pay attention to who walks alone, notice who is at the back or the front of the group, and use these small windows of time to engage with the young people who may need you the most.

Between 1995 and 2009, I co-led twelve bus tours around Israel. Nine of them were one-week trips with college students, while three were month-long trips with high school students. During these trips, I eventually realized that a significant portion of the magic of these trips happened during the endless hours we were driving from location to location.

Most days, we were up early and traveled until the evening. For most members of staff and participants, the bus rides were opportunities to catch up on sleep. When I walked along the aisle of the bus, however, I soon discovered that some participants were awake and eager to talk about their experiences. Some of the most intensive learning during those tours took place during bus time. Participants asked questions that couldn't be asked, let alone answered, during structured tours and seminars. As well as engaging in some fascinating conversations, I inevitably became privy to important conversations that informed my understanding of the group dynamics, which helped me to get to know the participants and respond appropriately to roommate conflicts or to those with greater needs.

As the bus example illustrates, it's important to **be visible**. In Gaza, we specifically hired staff who lived within walking distance of each program venue to increase the chances that they would end up walking along the same routes as our participants, nudging them toward a different kind of connection.

Consider, too, how you can **schedule informal time**. Incorporate longer breaks and transitions into your program schedule. As the work in Gaza illustrates, making informal time a part of every single day embeds it into the consciousness of each participant and member of staff. Often it's only over time, as the connections form, that the real power of informal time makes itself apparent.

Finally, take a few minutes and **ask the young people** you work with what kind of time with you is most important to them and why. You may be surprised by what they say. "Hanging out" may not seem like an activity, but it could well be the time that they need you the most.

CHAPTER TWO

KNOW THEIR STORY

. . . .

In November 1995, I was wrapping up a fascinating season of teaching in Maine. It was intense work and I loved it. Fall was ending and our busy season was winding down. The work remained interesting, but the prospect of living alone through a Maine winter gave me pause.

After a rushed job search, I landed a position as a resident adviser at the Brush Ranch School (BRS) in the Pecos National Forest, about forty-five minutes outside of Santa Fe. I packed everything into my car, and following short pit stops in Cleveland and Saint Louis, I pulled into the snow-dusted BRS parking lot in early January 1996. This was eight years before I began to consciously consider the impact of Vital Connections. At the time, I wasn't able to articulate what the events I'm about to describe meant to me. Yet even then, I knew they were important.

BRS was a residential school for adolescents exhibiting

a host of behavioral challenges, often combined with moderate to significant learning disabilities. There were students with Tourette's syndrome, attention disorders, and a range of other cognitive, emotional, and interpersonal struggles. Many of these students were terribly misunderstood and weren't functioning well in their home communities. There weren't many places left for them to go. The venue had originally been a summer camp, and most of the structures from that period remained in use. Log cabins dotted the banks of the Pecos River, and a wooden bridge connected the two sides of the property. Several buildings had been constructed as classrooms, but much remained the same. Members of staff ate in the dining hall and lived with our students in the cabins.

I arrived in the middle of the school year, replacing a departing staff member in the cabin with the oldest students, who were between sixteen and nineteen years old. My predecessor had been well-liked by his students, but he was fired by the school administration for egregious behavior. As a resident adviser, I was responsible for everything related to my students' day-to-day living and well-being. This meant living in the cabin with them, managing their wake-up times and bedtimes, and planning and facilitating after-school activities. I worked the weekend shift—Thursday to Monday—before handing off my cabin to my co-adviser, who then moved in for the weekday shift.

Working at BRS was one of the hardest things I've ever done and one of the most amazing. My six students were tough and intimidating. At least three of them were bigger than me in every way: height, weight, and personality. They had been at BRS for several years. In both healthy and unhealthy ways, this group of six ran the school.

This became abundantly clear to me as early as my very first shift. After brief introductions in the cabin entrance and a wave goodbye from my administrative director, my students ushered me down one of the hallways into the common room. They had rearranged the couch and chairs into a row, except for one chair they had pulled out for me. They directed me to the single chair and proceeded to occupy the couch and the other chairs, facing me like a panel of judges.

Clearly, they weren't trying to welcome me cordially to BRS. They were asserting their seniority and authority. As I sat there trying to convey my most confident and authoritative self, they launched into a well-planned and detailed overview of the nuances of residential life at BRS, along with the various dos and don'ts of working with them. It was both overwhelming and impressive. One thing was immediately clear: working with them was going to require all of my influence and negotiation skills.

The school operated on principles of behavior modification. This consisted of a complex and detailed points system. Every day, each student earned or lost points, based on their behavior. This began when they woke up—on time or late—and continued throughout the day, right up until lights out. The points they earned correlated with different levels, ranging between zero and four. Over time, students sustaining higher levels of behavior were rewarded with greater privileges and freedoms, including the opportunity to attend off-site trips and participate in unsupervised activities. Those with fewer points faced greater restrictions.

With one exception, each of my students consistently hovered around levels zero and one. This meant that they were subject to twenty-four-hour supervision and experienced tremendous restrictions on their activities. For them, and for me, this *sucked*. They missed out on numerous enrichment opportunities, they weren't allowed to leave their cabin without a member of staff, they could not have friends visit the cabin, and they were severely limited in the times they could venture outside school property. Most of the time, they were trapped on campus, permitted only the minimum scheduled activities on the weekends, and constantly bumped up against the limitations associated with their low scores. It was a vicious circle: bored and frustrated, they drifted into messy situations, became angry or apathetic, and often lost the ability to self-regulate, further prolonging the constraints on their behavior.

Cohabiting with a cabin of struggling adolescents for three-and-a-half days each week is one of the wildest, most surreal experiences I've ever had. They were saddled not only with the long list of challenges usually associated with navigating adolescence and early adulthood but also with significant learning challenges and the stigma of being labeled "dumb" and "special education." On top of this were the cumulative effects of months or years of having their behavior assessed to be at level zero. Imagine that before leaving your home every day, the last thing you see is a sheet of paper, tacked up by the front door, with a big zero next to your name.

Working the weekend shift often felt like a dead zone for programming. During the week, students were in school most of the day and the residential staff ran one evening program. From Friday night to Sunday night, however, I and other members of staff on my shift were responsible for two full days of programming. I was deep in my activities guy phase at the time, so I loved this challenge, but I faced the additional obstacle of trying to engage my six students in any activity beyond playing board games—which was, in practice, an excuse to sit in the cabin and do nothing.

One staff member ran a regular poetry club, the last activity I expected my students to show an interest in. Very soon after I arrived, however, I found myself bundled up against the snow, walking with them to poetry club accompanied by almost every one of my students. Little by little, they began to share some of their poetry with me. It was beautiful.

Eventually, in the spring, a few students approached me and other members of staff with the idea of hosting an open mic coffee house event. Some of the students in my cabin took charge of designing and decorating the space. They built candleholders out of soda cans and taped garbage bags over every window in the room for "atmosphere." We brought in a sound system, set up chairs, and cleared a space for the stage.

The entire school attended. Almost every student in my cabin took a turn at the microphone and shared some of their work. What they revealed was moving, inspiring, and at times heart-wrenching. It was adolescent angst at its rawest and most truthful. By the time the garbage bags were ripped down and the doors of the coffee house closed, I saw my students, and many other students at the school, in a completely different light. This was not the first time I had come to know a young person through a piece of work they had written or performed. That night, however, was especially profound. As each student graced the stage and spoke, their words expanded my appreciation for them and my ability to understand the very rough road their lives had taken.

I felt overwhelmed by a heavy dose of compassion, which struck directly at my heart. I remember sitting in the back of the coffee house, feeling each of my students far more deeply than I had imagined possible. These were young people I had exhausted every ounce of patience, care, and skill I possessed in trying to reach. When that failed, on occasion I had resorted to raising my voice or—worse—walking away.

Sitting in the makeshift coffee house, I reflected on how I'd been interacting with each of them. I considered the strategies and tactics I had used and the times I'd given up trying. Hearing their words challenged me to reconsider my fundamental understanding of how I knew them and think again about the way I approached my work with them. It was startling to realize how much I didn't know about each of them and how important it was to learn everything I could.

It would be years before I pieced together what this event and my time at BRS really meant to me. It was a striking moment of connection that shone like a beacon, but it happened long before I had a framework for understanding Vital Connections. Yet even then, I experienced an important shift in my work with young people. Their stories, all of them, mattered much more than I had understood. They opened up a window into parts of their lives I had never imagined and forever changed the way I saw them.

That night, despite having lived with these students for several months, I realized how much I didn't know about their stories. As I listened to their words, I was humbled by the realization of how much it mattered for me to try to get to know them better.

CHOOSING TO CONNECT

One of the students in my cabin at BRS, Mikey, enjoyed whittling. Living in a national forest, we had access to a lot of wood. It was an activity he could focus on for long stretches of time, and it was something that gave him a sense of competency and esteem.

For many reasons, however, it was difficult for me to allow Mikey to whittle. The school had a strict policy about weapons on campus, which applied to both students and staff. A knife or blade of any kind was undoubtedly a weapon. Mikey, like most of my students, oscillated between level zero and level one on the school's behavioral points system, meaning that even if there was a possibility of allowing him to possess a knife, he was forbidden from such activities. Worse, my relationship with Mikey was tenuous, making it even harder for me to trust him with a knife.

For months, I complied with school policy on this issue. It seemed a simple decision. The only thing that gave me pause for thought was the regular appearance of knives and power tools in packages addressed to Mikey. Approximately once a month, someone in his family mailed him a package containing some sort of tool. Month after month, I confiscated these items and turned them over to the school. Naturally, this did not endear me to Mikey.

One month, however, I suddenly reversed my decision. After months of confiscating the knives and tools in Mikey's packages, I looked up at him as he received his mail and saw him seething, already prepared for disappointment and frustration. On the spot, I decided to let him keep it. At the time, I knew the decision felt right, but I had no clear rationale to explain why. Only years later could I articulate the reasons behind my choice.

Working out the rules of engagement took quite a lot of negotiation, but eventually we settled on a plan. I kept the blade when he wasn't using it. He only worked with it under supervision and at certain times. The result? Mikey began whittling on the weekends. There were no injuries. He never raised the blade in aggression. He kept it in perfect condition. He was happier, and I experienced him as easier to work with—all good outcomes. I supported the school's overall policy, but I saw something in Mikey that caused me to reconsider. Despite many failed attempts, I had gotten to know him quite well over several months. The stories he told me convinced me both that he needed the opportunity to whittle and that he could handle the responsibility, no matter what the school rules said. My perspective had shifted, and it happened because I had come to know him so much better.

KNOWING THEIR STORY OPENS A DOOR

One of our most foundational human needs is to be known. I'm always saddened to think about how many people live their lives in severe isolation, unknown by others. There's a very real reason why solitary confinement is one of the most devastating forms of punishment we've ever invented. It drains a person of the vitality that comes of being known by others. It relentlessly inflicts the pain that comes from disappearing from everyone else's awareness.

In both my career and personal life, I have encountered many young people who feel misunderstood and unlovable. They don't feel that anyone really knows them, and in some cases, they doubt that their existence matters to anyone else. Tragically, the young people who could benefit most from being known by caring adults are often those trapped in patterns of behavior that exacerbate their sense of isolation. They put their defenses up and make it difficult to know them. They may also display behaviors that test an adult's commitment to get to know them. My cabin of students certainly did this to me when I first arrived. What do we do as adults? In most cases, we respond as they expect us to, with discipline, distance, or other isolating approaches.

We issue time-outs to children, pushing them away from us and sending the message that they are unworthy of our interest and attention. As they grow older, we send them to detention, which often includes sitting in silence. As the pattern escalates, we suspend them, expel them, and eventually incarcerate them. All in response to their best efforts to navigate the challenges they're facing, challenges with which they could probably use the assistance of a caring adult who knows what they're going through.

Regrettably, this was a central feature of how the system at BRS operated. It blocked access to caring adults and peers for the students who probably needed them the most. It left them out of the loop of crucial social interaction and support. Level zero status denied these students opportunities to be known.

To be known, young people need opportunities to be in the presence of caring adults in contexts that allow both adult and young person to build a sense of rapport and comfort with each other. This is a major reason why making time at the right time is the first Vital Connection. Once we start making time for the young people who need us, we create the opportunity to explore the second Vital Connection with a young person, **knowing their story**.

When we know someone, we give them a place in our world, in our mind, and eventually in our heart. When that happens, we start to care about them in the ways that they need to be cared for.

WEAVING THE SOCIAL FABRIC

In his book *Vital Friends*, Tom Rath describes a research project in which he participated in the United States in the early 1990s. It was called Project Recovery.[6] The aim of the research was to better understand the circumstances that led to people becoming chronically homeless and the factors that allowed some people who had been chronically homeless to achieve stable housing.

Prior to the study, mental illness, a history of abuse, and drug and alcohol addiction were all perceived as some of the common causes of chronic homelessness. The study concluded, however, that these were mostly secondary factors. The most important root cause of a descent into chronic homelessness was the destruction of a person's social fabric. It could start with the death of a spouse, a move away from a close community, or some other major event that erodes a person's social fabric. The other factors listed above were often present, but while a person

---

6   Tom Rath, *Vital Friends: The People You Can't Afford to Live Without* (New York: Gallup Press, 2006).

remained connected to and supported by others, these risk factors would be effectively mitigated.

The study concluded that the single most important factor in helping reverse a person's situation was the reconstitution of their social fabric. This could take the form of a family member, a friend, or a caseworker, someone who decided to stay in this person's life and not let them slip out of contact.

I think about this study regularly. Perhaps more than any other research I've read, it makes the case that Vital Connections play an essential role in all our lives, not only the lives of children and adolescents. Even as adults, we all need other caring figures. We all need someone who shows up for us, who expects us to show up, and who wants to get to know us, no matter what our circumstance.

Alcoholics Anonymous (AA) understands this principle well, as evidenced by the role of the "sponsor" in their twelve-step recovery program. To work through the twelve steps, a member must work with a willing sponsor who supports them through the program. When the pain that may push a person toward pouring a drink surfaces, they know that there is at least one person out there who knows their story and will listen, and show up, no matter what. We all need someone who keeps us on their mind, who wonders how we are doing, and who wants to know how our lives are progressing.

This is beautifully illustrated by a study undertaken by John Heritage and Jeffrey D. Robinson, two American conversation analysts. Their study, published in 2007, explored the consequences when doctors altered one word in their dialogue with patients during routine visits.[7] Heritage and Robinson instructed one group of doctors to say, "Is there anything else we need to take care of today?" The other group was told to ask, "Is there *something* else we need to take care of today?" That simple one-word difference resulted in a statistically significant increase in patients reporting fresh concerns to their doctors.

This change might seem minor, but looked at through the lens of Vital Connections, it's profound. The word *something* sends a powerful message from the doctor to the patient, conveying to the patient that the doctor thinks there could be more to their story. It's a subtle but important encouragement to share more.

Why does this matter? It's a reminder of how important it is to *truly* believe that each young person has a story worth hearing. They have *something* important to tell about who they are and how they got to where they are.

---

7   John Heritage, Jeffrey D. Robinson, Marc N. Elliot, Megan Beckett, and Michael Wilkes, "Reducing Patients' Unmet Concerns in Primary Care: The Difference One Word Can Make," *Journal of General Internal Medicine* 22, no. 10 (2007): 1429-1433 (https://www.ncbi.nlm.nih.gov/pmc/articles/PMC2305862/).

PUTTING IT INTO PRACTICE: KNOWING THEIR STORY

When we commit to getting to know the young people we work with, the best place to begin is with the basics.

The most essential place to start is to **learn their name**. To be known by our name is to feel that we exist and that we are memorable to another person. Take the time to learn each young person's name, including how they pronounce it and any nicknames they like to be known by. This skill sounds almost too basic, but I cannot overstate how powerful a feeling it can be to a young person to have an adult call them by their chosen name. Ask them how *they* pronounce it. Write it down if you have to, and practice until you get it right.

I am not naturally talented at remembering names, but I've learned a few tricks that help. Whenever I can, I study the names of young people I work with in advance. I memorize attendance sheets or class photos. The first time I meet a young person, I ask them three or four times to tell me their name until I get it right. When I take attendance, I pause a few seconds to match the name of each participant with their face. I create positive associations with each person to help me identify them as a unique individual. I test myself in front of them. When all else fails, I make a rule that everyone must wear a name tag on which their first name is written in big letters, including me.

The second level of knowing a young person is the **basic**

facts about their life. These facts include such information as age, grade, language(s) spoken, where they live, family structure, and interests. These can be learned from some good-old question and answer. A little gentle, surface-level inquiry goes a long way. At first, you may be met with a lot of yesses and nos. No matter; at this level, you're still acquiring valuable information. Depending on where you work, you also may be able to access participant profiles, bios, or even more substantive records of a young person's basic story.

The third level is made up of your **observations and impressions.** When you spend time with a young person, you can start to form a more robust and layered picture of who they are. You may notice some of their strengths and weaknesses or observe how they handle stress and challenges. Perhaps you see that they get angry easily or that they have a dry sense of humor. You may notice that they tend to act as a peacemaker among peers or that they talk in great detail about their plans for their future. As you absorb this information, you will form deeper impressions about the kind of person they are, their competencies, and their aspirations.

It's important to avoid falling into the trap of letting impressions become fixed conclusions or generalizations, or worse, labeling. By definition, an impression is a feeling or opinion about someone based on limited evidence. We form impressions about other people all the time. At their best, impressions become conversation starters that we use to ask better questions and gather more information about a person, to help us paint the fullest picture possible. At their worst, impressions restrict the lens through which we see someone and fuel stereotypes and prejudice. As youth workers, however, we have a sacred responsibility to use the impressions we may be forming about a young person to drive more curiosity and inquiry, and to assume there is so much more to know about their story.

The fourth level is what I call the **deeper story.** This usually emerges only over time. The deeper story is comprised of a young person's hopes, fears, challenges, goals, and aspirations. When you know a young person's deeper story, you should begin to gain a better understanding and deeper appreciation of the unique context of their life. Context is the setting young people spend their time in, including their home, school, and social and community life. Context shapes behavior and outlook and is an essential part of knowing their full story.

When you work with a young person over time, you will discover that as you grow to know them more deeply, the sum of who they are begins to feel like more than simply the parts of their story. You will gain a genuine, rich, and candid picture of them. And if you do this well, it won't feel intrusive to that young person or to you. It will simply feel like the progression of a real relationship.

None of this is to suggest that you should be digging into each young person's darkest history or secrets. You can do tremendous work with many young people equipped with only the most basic information about them. In certain situations, you may also need to adhere to professional guidelines and boundaries that prevent you from knowing young people as deeply as you might like.

Nonetheless, there are many occasions when knowing more about a young person will aid you in understanding how best to interact with them and potentially amplify the impact you can have on them. Take the time to *try* to get to know each young person you work with. Find an aspect of their life that fuels your genuine curiosity, then pause and give your full and undivided attention to their story.

This type of getting-to-know-each-other interaction between a young person and an adult is less frequent than you may think. Some of what you hear may make your heart ache, or you may feel ill-equipped to help them the way you wish you could. If that happens, remember Kwinji. Unless you are trained in a specialized service and have the mandate to intervene, you may not be able to provide them with everything they need. If you get to know their story, however, you may be able to show them critical compassion or refer them to a person or organization that can help.

For a young person living with the pain of bullying, grief, trauma, or isolation, feeling that they are known by even one adult can be the difference between picking up the phone to ask for help and picking up a bottle of pills or a gun. All of us, adults included, do better when we have caring adults in our lives who can wrap us up in an open, supportive, and protective social fabric.

There are already many workshops and books that teach people about storytelling. One of the greatest and least appreciated skills, however, is **story-listening**. Story-listening is a commitment to bear full witness to a young person's story, however much or little they want to share with you at any given time. When you story-listen, you make the choice to shine a gentle, curious, and empathetic spotlight on that young person.

What is the right space for story-listening? It's the space where they can be most comfortable. That could be around a table, on a walk, playing catch, or on a drive. Eye contact can be important, but it's not essential. For some young people, sustained eye contact may cause them to shut down, while sitting side by side in the front seats of a car or on a bench could be exactly what's needed for them to open up.

When you story-listen, you allow the young person to set the tone and pace for their story, even if you think you know where it's going. You commit to not skipping ahead. Silence can be your ally here. This means delaying your response or reaction for a few long, slow seconds. When I say nothing immediately in reply, it's amazing how often a young person finds more to say. If you are looking for something to say, the three most important words in story-listening are, "Tell me more." You may need to ask the same question more than once or pose a series of yes/no questions to get the story going. Some stories start with a gushing flow of information, while others may be a slow trickle.

Story-listening only works when you decide to commit that individual young person to your memory. This Vital Connection is forged from choosing to remember this young person—their name, their age, their birthday, their favorite class in school, the fact that they are usually late for practice because they take two buses to get there. Creating memories of their story allows you to pick up where you left off and gradually build a broader and deeper understanding of that young person.

At its core, story-listening is an exercise in building trust. It may take many conversations before you piece together a young person's story, but you can always take the opportunity to reinforce the belief that every young person you work with has an important story to tell, that they have *something* more to tell you.

Plato spoke the truth when he said, "You can discover more about a person in an hour of play than in a year of conversation." For some young people, talking may not be their favored medium. You may find that a young person you work with prefers a **nonverbal medium for storytelling**. There are so many other ways to tell a story that don't involve a one-on-one conversation: drawing, painting, dancing, creating music, and, of course, poetry.

Play cards or a board game together, throw a Frisbee, shoot hoops, sing a song, dance, get out and run. There is as much to learn about a young person through activity as there is through conversation. Sometimes talking is overrated.

As we move into part two of this book, we'll start to explore more intricate and involved Vital Connections. The following two chapters are packed with material and, consequently, are the longest chapters in the book. Think of this book like a bell curve. We're now entering the bulk of the curve, where the majority of the work and research has taken place, so there's a lot to share.

That's not to say that one Vital Connection is more important than any other. Each one is essential in its own way.

The key to using Vital Connections effectively is to recognize what the young person in front of you needs right now and to do what you can to meet those needs.

PART TWO

BELIEF AND CONVERSATION

Chapter Three

BELIEVE THEY CAN SUCCEED

. . . .

In summer 2008, it felt like all of Addis Ababa was under construction. I was in Ethiopia consulting to the Worldwide Orphans Foundation (WWO), an organization working to improve the health and well-being of orphans around the world. WWO had been working in Ethiopia since 2005, operating a clinic and a school to serve orphans and vulnerable children, many infected with or affected by HIV. My mission was the same as it had been in Thailand in 2004: design a camp program, train local staff and international volunteers to run it, and oversee its initial implementation.

WWO's ambition was to create a camp experience that could play a role in bridging the summer gap. Many of the children who called an orphanage home struggled during the summer months. When they were away from the structure and rhythm of their school schedules, it was harder to adhere to their medication and meal routines. It was more difficult for medical staff to visit them and provide them with regular monitoring and support. Sustaining the health of any child living with HIV is challenging. These factors complicated that task further.

Some mornings, I caught a ride with other staff to the school grounds in the center of the city. Other days, I walked. Surrounding the numerous buildings under construction were huge, teetering towers of wooden scaffolding, nailed and screwed together, looking as though they might topple over with a mild breeze. Roads running through the city, which started off wide and paved, ended abruptly in dirt. My walk took me through blocks of shops and street vendors, across and alongside a major road. After a short climb up an embankment, I banged on a dented metal gate, waiting for the security guard to open the small door and usher me in.

Any visitor standing outside the gate would have had no idea what was inside. The school was enclosed in a compound, with walls separating it from adjacent buildings and a metal gate at the front entrance. As I stepped through, I crossed into another world. I was greeted with the riotous and wonderful sight of fifty children, each one between six and eight years old, running, jumping, talking, and laughing, both with each other and with the staff. The courtyard, our makeshift playground, was too small for so many people, which amplified the intensity of the energy. When I arrived, between three and thirty of the children invariably stopped whatever they were doing and sprinted over to greet me.

At the time, I flattered myself that their joyous interest in high-fiving and hugging me reflected my great skill as a camp counselor. The truth, however, was that their enthusiasm and love was so great and indiscriminate that they did the same for almost every visitor.

One day, when I stepped through the gate, I was carrying several bags: my regular camp backpack full of paperwork, a sweatshirt, hat, and water bottle, and a large, very heavy duffel. As usual, I was met with a flurry of smiles, shouts, and greetings. Soon the excited campers dispersed, except for two who lingered beside me, conversing rapidly in Amharic.

I pride myself on learning languages quite quickly. I start with the basics and try to pinpoint the words and phrases that are most relevant to the context in which I'm working. I scribble everything into tiny notebooks I carry in a pocket and use every opportunity I can to practice what I'm learning, no matter how poor my accent or pronunciation. It's not elegant, but it works.

Two or three weeks into my time in Addis, I had learned

a few pages' worth of words and phrases such as "thank you," "excellent," "amazing," "incredible," "bathroom," and "ready, set, go!" I could also count from one to five, and I knew the Amharic word for "popcorn." Despite my fledgling skills, I was immediately out of my depth as the two young campers chatted away beside me. I had absolutely no idea what they were saying.

It quickly became clear that their interest was directed more toward my giant bag than toward me personally. With a combination of guesswork and exaggerated hand gestures, I soon discovered that they wanted to help carry my duffel bag. Although I tried to convey to them that the bag was far too heavy for two small children, they were undeterred. In the face of their giant smiles and dogged persistence, I caved in and humbly stepped aside.

Immediately, they grabbed at the handles and base of the bag. Unable to lift it from the ground, they began to drag it across the concrete playground, tugging and grunting with all their might. They worked together, pushing, pulling, and seemingly willing the bag forward. As it scraped along the ground, small fibers from the bottom of the bag were shredded. Finally, they delivered the bag to the next building, about twenty feet from the entrance. They looked up at me, simultaneously exhausted and exhilarated by their success. I thanked them profusely, and they raced back to play with their fellow campers.

Early in my youth development career, I picked up a tradition that I've since kept alive in most of the programs where I've worked. It's a daily ritual aimed at recognizing participants who make meaningful contributions to the program's culture, community, or spirit. Each day, we acknowledge two or three participants in a brief, fun public ceremony. We also ensure that over the course of a week or month of the program, each child has the chance to receive recognition.

That day, it was easy to decide whom to celebrate. At lunchtime, we called these two powerful luggage handlers by name, and I shared the story of their exertions. "I appreciate it when people in our camp community seek out ways to help others," I said. "They are team players. That's being a good friend at camp." We cheered. We sang. They each donned a jersey we had fashioned into a makeshift uniform of honor. Then everyone returned to the serious business of camp.

The following morning, I once again opted to walk to camp, this time carrying only my backpack. Approaching the gate, I heard the unmistakable sounds of informal time in action. The gate opened, the guard and I exchanged a smile and a greeting, and I stepped into the courtyard. The instant the door opened, children swarmed me. At first, I thought I was merely the recipient of their typical daily greeting. I soon realized, however, that they were all reaching for anything they could help me carry! Within a few seconds, my backpack was peeled off my shoulders. Next, they removed my scarf, and as I glanced down, I saw tiny hands attempting to untie my shoes. Everything I owned that wasn't buttoned or zipped to my person was swiftly taken from me and delivered quickly and efficiently to the steps of the main building.

When the campers dispersed, I retied my shoes and collected my belongings. As I did so, I reflected on what had just taken place. The two minutes of acknowledgment we shared the previous day had triggered a flash flood of helpfulness. As I thought about it, I realized that I should have anticipated the powerful impact the praise would have. Young people, especially children of the age of those campers, are working hard to figure out how they fit into the world. They pay close attention to the actions and reactions of adults. If their behavior is met with frowns, they may conclude that it is not desired. If they receive smiles, interest, and encouragement, they may decide to repeat whatever they're doing.

We publicly praised two campers for helping me carry my bag, so naturally other children became motivated to experiment with the same behavior. It was an exceptionally strong response in that we inadvertently activated an entire rugby squad of helpful children. Since then, I've replayed that experience many times. It conveys the power of praise. Yet, I think there's another meaning. The episode above also serves as a gateway into a deeper understanding of how caring adults can influence and shape young people.

A TANK FULL OF SELF-EFFICACY

Starting around age three or four, children are on a developmental path to forge their self-efficacy. Psychologist Albert Bandura defines self-efficacy as a belief in one's ability to accomplish specific tasks or succeed in given situations. Self-efficacy contributes to self-esteem, self-confidence, and self-identity. Young people with a strong sense of self-efficacy set goals, approach challenges, and cope with setbacks more effectively than those with a poor sense of self-efficacy. Self-efficacy also plays an important role in the development of character. And it is fundamental in shaping how young people make decisions.

Self-efficacy is constantly shaped by new experiences and interactions. A key part of a child's development is exploring and engaging in new experiences and testing their capacity to learn and adapt. This process goes on in almost everything a child does, from running and climbing to learning language and making friends. Each challenge they face has the potential to influence their sense of competence and confidence.

As our sense of efficacy grows, we become more willing to try new things, to reach out, and to ask for help. Our fear of failure becomes less prevalent, and we become more capable of learning from our disappointments. We believe in our own competence and anticipate success. When we experience setbacks, we face them with more confidence.

Self-efficacy, however, is not an either/or phenomenon. Rather, it's best described as a point along a continuum. We all experience ebbs and flows in our sense of self-efficacy. A useful metaphor, often used in youth development work, is that our sense of self-efficacy is like a tank of gas—or as Jim Thompson, founder of the Positive Coaching Alliance, describes it, an emotional tank. When our tanks are full, we see ourselves as capable, competent, and confident. We positively identify with statements such as, "I don't give up," "I try new things," and "I make healthy choices." Young people operating with a full emotional tank are filled with optimism, power, perseverance, and energy. Those operating with empty tanks may be beset with pessimism, self-doubt, and even shame.

The contents of our emotional tanks fluctuate from day to day. Yet each of us also operates at a baseline of self-efficacy, a level to which we routinely return. Tragically, far too many young people walk around with chronically low or empty emotional tanks and correspondingly low levels of self-efficacy. One of our most important tasks is to assess the levels of self-efficacy of the young people we work with and do what we can to help them fill their tanks. It's our responsibility to act with a relentless commitment to providing evidence in support of filling their emotional tanks.

This approach is fundamental to the third Vital Connection, **believing they can succeed**. It begins with your conviction that a young person truly *can* succeed and encompasses a host of techniques you can use to help them develop a solid, positive sense of their own efficacy. As caring adults, we have a special ability to infuse our belief into young people's thoughts and feelings, influencing how they perceive themselves. It happened with the young campers in Addis Ababa, and I've seen it on countless other occasions. For a young person struggling with their self-efficacy, it might be easier to avoid a challenge than face it head-on. If they fall into this pattern of avoidance, their self-efficacy may drop so far that they begin to withdraw, hiding from challenges to protect their fragile self-esteem and confidence.

Turning this pattern of avoidance around, especially for young people who have heard too many times, from peers and adults, that they are not capable, takes a specific set of approaches. A young person who has repeatedly experienced painful failures or been told that they are "bad" may believe that they are not going to succeed before they even try. In the next segment of this book, I'll discuss how we can support young people in filling their emotional tanks and building their self-efficacy.

PUTTING IT INTO PRACTICE: BELIEVING THEY CAN SUCCEED

The best part of this Vital Connection is that many varied and powerful ways exist to bring believing they can succeed into your work. Some of these techniques will take only a few seconds of your time, while others require a more in-depth approach. What matters is your commitment to providing regular, meaningful, and genuine infusions of your belief in the young people in your care.

All of us possess unconscious—and sometimes conscious—biases that affect how we see the capabilities of young people. It's easy to become caught in the trap of playing favorites. Alternatively, we may withhold our positive regard for a young person we find more challenging to work with or whom we hold a bias toward. Whatever our personal biases, it is crucial that we instill our belief in the capacities of every single young person we work with.

In this book, I want to highlight four specific ways to show young people you believe they can succeed. These are **affirmations, praise, questions**, and **storytelling**.

USING AFFIRMATIONS

An affirmation is an offer of emotional support or encouragement, which can take the form of words, gestures, or actions. Affirmations tend to be very brief, usually occupying only a few seconds of time. Yet even in these brief moments, we can communicate a great deal about our belief in a young person. It's remarkable how much impact the right few words or gestures of encouragement can have at the right moment. There are many types of affirmations we can offer a young person. When promoting the specific goal of self-efficacy, however, some words and actions have more weight than others.

The first and easiest type of affirmation is simply to say, frequently and sincerely, "**I believe in you**." Remember, we are aiming to influence the belief systems of the young people we work with. If they are experiencing self-doubt, they may need to hear a different voice than their own. They need to hear your voice. For many young people, receiving this basic affirmation is a rare event. When we give this affirmation, we help them reconsider their own capabilities and efforts.

Many young people have suffered with self-doubt and anxiety for so long that they are convinced they are not only failing at certain activities but also failing as people. For these young people, consider appending the phrase "no matter what" to your affirmations. Young people may need to know that someone believes in them, win or lose. Saying, "I believe in you, no matter what," sends the message that their effort is more crucial than their performance. In these few words, you convey that your belief in them is unconditional.

In addition to our words, we can also deliver **affirmations through actions**. The first way to do this is to simply show up for what matters to them. Sometimes we all want, and can benefit from, a supportive audience. Even an audience of one can suffice. When a young child starts to explore their surroundings, they often look back to see if their caregiver is watching and supporting them. When that child looks back at their caregiver and sees them smile, cheer, or offer an encouraging wave, they receive an infusion of self-belief. When they see frowning, anxious adults, the message we send is that we don't trust their self-efficacy. And if the caregiver isn't there, they receive the message that there is no one in their corner. This doesn't apply only to children. Tweens and teens can benefit equally from seeing you at the events and experiences that matter to them. When we show up for young people, we convey that we believe in them.

Another way to communicate the same message is to offer them a high-five, fist bump, or hug before, during, or after a challenging activity. In Vital Connections' workshops, I love to lead an exercise that gives participants an opportunity to develop this skill. I ask them to form pairs and stand back to back. Then I ask them to imagine that they are working with a young person whom they believe in and who is taking on a new challenge. Their task is to demonstrate their belief. The catch? The young person is far away from them, and they must show their belief across this distance. Perhaps the young person is playing tennis and learning to adapt their footwork to make a backhand return. I count to three; then each person spins around and shows their partner what they would do.

Some people pump their arms above their heads. Others jump up and down, or cheer and shout. Many wear huge beautiful smiles and other encouraging facial expressions. After a few moments, I stop them and instruct them to once again turn back to back. Then I ask them to turn around again, this time *doubling* their level of affirmation. People go wild. The point of the exercise is not simply that louder is better. It's that some young people have experienced so many setbacks and discouraging comments that they may need larger gestures of affirmation.

GIVING MEANINGFUL PRAISE

Great praise comes down to two basic elements: first, knowing **what to praise**, and second, knowing **how to give praise** in a way that delivers maximum impact. When both of these elements are part of your praise, it drops into a young person's emotional tank and stays there. Let's start with the "what" of giving meaningful praise.

Remember, our aspiration with praise, as part of this Vital Connection, is specifically to enhance self-efficacy. To do this, we need to align our praise with our definition of self-efficacy. Our praise needs to provide that young person with additional, irrefutable evidence that they have what it takes to accomplish the challenge they face. If they can't succeed in a given situation, the praise must encourage them to believe that they can return to try again. Therefore, great praise should target the following:

Effort: This is the pure energy it takes to reach a goal, or simply to show up, again and again. However, effort is more than participation. The type of effort that should be targeted for praise occurs when a young person tries harder than they have before, applies their energy to a new approach, expends themselves fully in an activity, or considers quitting, yet ultimately decides to try again. Other words we can use when praising effort include *persistence*, *grit*, *resilience*, and *commitment*.

Progress: It's easy to make the mistake of praising young people for their achievements. We celebrate the sporting victory or the academic grade. For the purposes of self-efficacy, it matters more to help the young person pay attention to how they are growing and learning. This means that we should focus on praising progress. Progress is almost always measurable, so we can provide young people with hard data about their expanding capabilities. Offer a young person an example of how they are getting better, no matter how small the increment. Other words we can use when praising progress include *improvement*, *growth*, *change*, and *development*.

Thoughtful Action: Thoughtful action involves thinking first, making a calculated assessment of a situation, and then pursuing a specific course. This is when young people learn the most. They think, they act, and then they experience the consequences. We can't always know what a young person is thinking, but sometimes we can speculate or discern it from their behavior. At other times, we can inquire. We can use praise to support their critical thinking and decision-making skills. Other words we can use when praising thoughtful action include *reflection*, *preparation*, *problem solving*, and *consideration*.

Doing the Right Thing: Even young children are faced with moments in their lives when they have the chance to do the right thing: to comfort a friend in need, to stand up for what matters to them, or simply to continue being the person they want to be, despite pressures to be someone they aren't. These moments are particularly powerful in shaping self-efficacy. They can deeply affect a young person's understanding of themselves and how they can impact the world around them. Other words we can use when praising doing the right thing include *courage*, *strength*, *empathy*, and *helpfulness*.

Effort, progress, thoughtful action, and doing the right thing are not the only characteristics worth praising, but they are worth prioritizing, due to the impact they can have on self-efficacy. The next question is *how* we give praise so that young people experience it as meaningful and effective. Great praise works when it's:

Accurate: Praise must reflect the reality of the situation. This means we must make an honest assessment and choose praise that is relevant, real, and truthful. Even young children can usually tell when an adult is sharing empty praise that is disconnected from the reality of a situation.

Specific: Gather specific evidence that supports the praise you want to offer. If you wish to praise a young person's efforts, what examples can you give them? If you want to detail their progress, do you have any information you can share that helps to make your case? Another aspect of specificity is to ensure that you provide enough information to help the young person make sense of the praise you give them.

Genuine: Whenever you share praise, it needs to emanate

from your heart. This means conveying, with your words, tone, and feelings, that you mean what you say. When you share genuine praise, the young person to whom you deliver it will likely experience it that way.

Here's an example of the distinction between good praise and great praise. Imagine a young person struggling with a math problem. He keeps getting stuck and starting over. Several times, you watch him erase his work and rewrite it, attempting to solve the problem.

Good praise would involve saying something like, "I'm proud of you; you're trying really hard." Great praise goes deeper. An example of great praise, in this context, would be, "I've been watching you working at this math problem for the past fifteen minutes, and I see that you've tried at least three or four different strategies to solve it. I can see you're frustrated, but it's impressive to me to see how persistent you are. You haven't given up, and you keep trying new approaches." The difference is that great praise includes a specific and accurate description of what the boy is doing, conveyed using language and tone that is heartfelt and sincere.

Now imagine the same boy at school, encountering a similar challenge during a math exam. He experiences the rising self-doubt that can accompany a difficult challenge. If he's received enough of the right kind of praise and his emotional tank is full, he may also hear a small, internal voice telling him, "Sometimes tough math problems take time. I may need to try a few different strategies before I get an answer." That message of self-efficacy may make the difference between persisting and giving up.

Here's a final technique to make your praise as meaningful as possible. **Ask them how the praise makes them feel.** Take the time to inquire about the impact of your praise. Clarify your intentions. Ask what they are hearing when you share your praise. Invite them to tell you what kind of praise is the most meaningful to them. Knowing how each young person receives praise will offer you rich insights into their sense of self-efficacy and allow you to make each piece of subsequent praise even more meaningful.

Here's an example of the power of great praise to help fill the emotional tank of a child. Newtown, Connecticut, was the scene of one of the worst school shootings in the history of the United States. Twenty first-graders and six adults were killed. The following summer, in 2013, Edgework was invited to work with their Parks and Recreation department. The department manages two-day camps for children in Newtown and Sandy Hook. We were asked to work with them to bring greater trauma sensitivity to their summer camps. Without a doubt, it's been one of our most meaningful engagements in all of Edgework's history.

After running a series of trainings and working with the camp leadership during the first year, I visited in late summer to observe how the camps were doing. I watched the counselors, mostly high school students from the community, playing with the campers in all kinds of activities, from swimming, to tag games, to drawing.

Beneath a large, sheltered pavilion, I noticed three boys playing soccer. This was a hectic space. There were campers and staff sitting at tables scattered around the pavilion. At first glance, kicking a ball around the space looked like a recipe for disaster. At any moment, I expected to see one of the boys kick the ball too hard and watch it crash into someone's head. I was itching to intervene and redirect their play, but I resisted.

As I watched, I realized that the boys were exercising incredible self-control. They always passed the ball gently. If a pass went awry, one of them sprinted after it and gathered it back. I was impressed. Part of my role at the camp was to train staff in the praise techniques described above, and I saw an opportunity to practice. I invited a couple of the staff to join me, and I asked the boys to come over.

"I want to tell you that I'm impressed," I said. "You have a lot of *composure*." I asked them whether they knew what composure was, and they replied that they didn't, so I explained further. "I've been watching you kick the ball around this pavilion for the last five minutes. It's quite a busy location, and it would have been easy to cause an accident. But I saw that when you kicked the ball, you did it gently, and if you missed it, you immediately chased after it. You had fun, without being disruptive or losing control of the soccer ball. That's called having composure. It's a really special skill to have." They smiled, shrugged, and then returned to their play.

Later, at the end of the day, I was observing a closing circle with one of the groups, whose members were discussing their highs and lows from the camp day. I was sitting a little bit behind the group. The counselor asked the campers in turn to share their favorite part of the day. One by one, each camper did so. Some enjoyed lunch, while others highlighted swimming, playing volleyball, or hanging out with friends.

One of the boys I had praised was in this group. When it was his turn to share his favorite part of his day, he said, "The best part of the day for me was when I learned that I have composure." He had spent an entire day immersed in countless games and activities, yet the experience that stayed with him was the ten seconds of praise.

ASKING POWERFUL QUESTIONS

For some young people, hearing an affirmation or praise

may not be enough to fill their emotional tank. They may attribute their success to luck or to circumstances outside their control, instead of seeing their own contributions and accomplishments. This may make it hard for them to understand how they can apply what they've learned to future endeavors.

Questions are both a way to bridge this gap and a useful tool for building self-efficacy. The key is to ask the *right* questions. Your aim here is to follow specific lines of questioning to uncover the parts of their story they may not be telling you—indeed, that may be hidden even from themselves.

Here's an example. Imagine a sixth-grader arriving at your after-school program, excited to tell you she scored a B on a math quiz. Previously, she has received C and D grades all year, so the improvement is a big deal. Yet she's struggling to believe that her success is a product of her own efforts. When you praise her approach and the qualities you've seen in her, she responds that she "got lucky," discounting her recent success. Her B is tangible evidence that she may be more capable than she thought; yet simultaneously, she is refusing to believe that evidence.

You praise her and affirm your belief in her capabilities. "I'm proud of you. I know how hard math has been for you this year. You must have worked really hard."

She shrugs, agreeing without truly allowing the praise in. "I did study hard this time," she admits.

Wanting to help her gain a fuller understanding of her own success, you ask, **"How did you do that?"**

She looks back at you, confused. "Huh?"

You repeat the question. "How did you do that?"

Again, she looks confused, but this time she seems slightly more reflective. "I guess I studied better this time," she says.

"I bet you did," you respond. "But I want to know *how* you did it. What was different this time? This is your first B all year."

If you hold your ground and keep exploring this question, you can eventually uncover the factors behind her academic victory. And in this discovery, you will help her see a part of herself that reveals what she did to achieve her coveted B. The odds are that she did much more than she realizes. Perhaps she created a study schedule or used flash cards. Maybe she asked her teacher or a classmate for help. Regardless of the specific techniques, the key is to help her understand that she took effective action to achieve a positive outcome in her life. If you can help her to become aware of that action, she may recognize more clearly the power she wields to influence her life in a positive direction. This in turn may encourage her to utilize some of her new strategies the next time she is studying.

The right question to ask in this context is, "How did you do that?" When you ask young people this question after they have achieved a success or improved in some activity or part of their life, it can unlock crucial actions, decisions, and self-beliefs that can help fuel greater self-efficacy. If we don't ask them to reflect on their behavior, we run the risk of allowing an important win to be brushed off as chance or luck. The win alone may not be sufficient to build self-efficacy. The win combined with the right line of questioning can help young people discover their own hidden capabilities.

Once you begin to ask young people how they have achieved success, you will find yourself pulled into fascinating conversations about their thought processes and actions, which can in turn fuel your—and their—belief that they can succeed. As you become more comfortable exploring this line of inquiry, you can expand it further, using questions such as, "Can you show me how you did that?" and "Can you teach me how to do that?"

A related question, which can help you and the young people you care for delve into their inner worlds, is, **"Why**

did you do that?" It needs to be said here that this question must be used carefully. It is often asked rhetorically, implying judgment of a young person's decisions, or interrogatively, as a request for justification of an action. In those circumstances, it will feel threatening and negative.

When asked with genuine curiosity and care, however, it can be an effective tool to help a young person reflect on their reasons for a decision. This conversation can open the door to a discussion about acting thoughtfully or doing the right thing, strengthening a young person's understanding of how they make decisions. These conversations can provide them with valuable insights to apply in similar situations in the future.

Powerful questions are useful when young people succeed, but they're also valuable when they have failed. You may say, "I know that didn't go the way you wanted. **What do you think happened?"** This can spark a discussion about what they can do differently next time. One final question, which I believe all youth workers should be ready to ask, is, **"How do you know you can't?"** This is particularly useful in situations where young people are ready to quit, yet you believe deeply that they can succeed. It is a direct challenge to the low perceptions they may hold of their self-efficacy. At times, young people may need us to challenge their focus on the negative and help them shift their focus to the reasons why they *can* succeed.

SHARING SOME OF YOUR STORIES

There are numerous ways to use stories when working with young people. You can share stories about other young people who have faced similar situations. You can reference stories from popular literature or media that reinforce a point you wish to make. In the specific context of aiming to promote self-efficacy, I encourage you to **tell stories about your own experiences**. Sharing moments of your own journey can help young people see their own experiences differently. The young people you work with may see you as a mentor or role model, which means that you are in a unique position to help them by sharing the challenges you have faced in becoming a competent, capable, and confident adult.

I'm not proposing that you primarily tell stories of your achievements, although there may be times when this is what a young person needs to hear. I'm talking about stories of your own successes *and* failures, which can help young people broaden their understanding of their own self-efficacy. For the purposes of this Vital Connection, these types of stories can be divided into six categories.

The first type of story is about **effort**. These are stories of times you've achieved something due to hard work and persistence. Sometimes young people can't see the adults they admire as people who have faced real challenges and worked hard to overcome them. They need to hear about what it took for us to get where we are today.

The second type of story is about **progress**. These stories focus on specific ways in which you've gradually grown and developed over time. Sometimes, these stories may feature prominent achievements, but what really matters is that you can speak openly about making progress, even if the story doesn't end with you getting where you wanted to go.

The third type of story focuses on experiences of **learning** how to do something, particularly something difficult. Very few important things in life are achieved without learning something difficult. Young people need to hear stories about this type of learning.

The fourth type of story concentrates on times of **failure** and the resilience that you developed as a result. How did you pick yourself up afterward? Or perhaps you languished in the doldrums for a while. How was that experience, and how did you finally recover?

The fifth type of story is about **future focus**, times when you have set goals and achieved them. What mindset do you adopt when you have an ambition? How do you remain hopeful or optimistic, despite the challenges you are facing?

The sixth and final story category focuses on **strengths**—times when you discovered something you were good at and enjoyed doing and how that made you feel. We need to show young people the power of focusing on strengths and how our understanding of our strengths shapes our sense of self-efficacy. For vulnerable young people, knowing even one of their own strengths can help fill an empty tank.

Speaking candidly about your own experiences and engaging in dialogue about the key themes or lessons of these stories can encourage young people to see their struggles as temporary and to feel that they, too, can bring about positive change in their lives. They may identify with certain stories, altering their self-perception and sense of self-efficacy. Some young people don't fully understand that as adults, we once struggled with very similar challenges to the ones they currently face—and that we still find life challenging. They need to hear our stories to help them see they are not alone.

Young people need the experience of caring adults in their lives who believe they can succeed. Without this level of attention, support, and mentorship, they are vulnerable to forming negative perceptions of their abilities, believing the worst that is said of them, and ultimately coming to resemble the negative characterizations of themselves they may see reflected in the eyes of others. When we exercise this third Vital Connection, we can play a role in helping them fill their emotional tanks and forge positive beliefs about their capabilities.

CHAPTER FOUR

SUPPORT VITAL CONVERSATIONS

* * * * * * *

In 1995, I worked for the Leadership Decisions Institute, now the Leadership School at Kieve-Wavus. The school is in Nobleboro, a small town near the Maine coast. Seventh- and eighth-graders came to the institute for a week at a time to attend classes focused on navigating adolescence. The class I taught was focused on peer relationships.

As I'm sure you can imagine, it was one of the most provoc- ative and sensitive classes on the schedule, generating a buzz among the students. We explored topics ranging from gender stereotypes to harassment. Invariably, the highlight of the week was the "talk show." All week, stu- dents submitted anonymous questions about sexuality and relationships, dropping their anonymous queries into an envelope that I safeguarded. They were encouraged to ask questions they were curious about, but too shy, nervous, or embarrassed to ask in public, especially in front of their peers.

Each week, I based the talk show on their questions. I also included some questions asked by students from other schools, which I felt warranted inclusion. The goal of the talk show was to foster an environment in which we could surface sensitive topics, provide reliable information, create more comfort and confidence talking openly with each other, and demonstrate to students that they weren't alone in their curiosity or confusion.

We sat on chairs in a circle, while I played the host. Some weeks I was "Lou-prah Winfrey." Other weeks, I was "Phil Dona-Lou." I sequenced the questions to create a natural flow, from lighter queries to deeper, more sensitive topics. The students played both audience and guests. I read each question out anonymously to the class, giving everyone the opportunity to jump in and provide a response. This created a dynamic in which the entire class could explore a topic, working together to try to help themselves and their classmates, without ever knowing who had asked the question.

After several weeks of facilitating the talk show, I was comfortable with the overall content and the format. There was one question, asked during those early weeks, that I felt needed to be included every week, whether a student wrote it down or not. The question was, "How do I know when it is OK to kiss someone I like?" On the surface, this is not a particularly risqué or taboo question. Yet I soon began to appreciate that for this age group, the path toward intimacy is beset with complications and important choices. Many adolescents—and even adults—find it difficult to openly and successfully navigate the topic of consent. I concluded that kissing had the potential to be a "gateway" toward better intimacy and relationships. If kissing was explicitly—not just implicitly—consensual, then maybe whatever happened next could also be consensual, comfortable, and safe.

When I asked this question, the students' initial response was almost always the same: a collective giggle coupled with a lot of excited whispers. After everyone calmed down, I asked the question again. At this point, I often received a variation of the following response: "If I'm at a movie, I do the 'arm move.' I bring my arm up and put it around their shoulder. If they don't move or fidget, I know that a kiss is probably next." Someone else might add, "Yeah! If they lean into you a little or brush your hand, you know they want to kiss you." I couldn't fault this logic. Indeed, I applied it on several occasions during my adolescence and well into adulthood. Yet it was missing something crucial. It left a lot of room for misunderstood actions and intentions, and it didn't explicitly convey consent.

After the students exhausted their initial ideas, I took the opportunity to advance the conversation. In dramatic talk show host fashion, I paused, then asked, "Could you ever just *ask* someone whether you could kiss them?" Every time I did this, the room erupted in expressions of disbelief. Some students waved their arms in the air, as if to push the idea out of their psychic space. "No way!" they shouted. "That's crazy." I sat there smiling, absorbing their intense reactions and waiting until they subsided. When the atmosphere quieted, I inquired whether anyone would like to share what was on their mind.

Almost always, one brave student would respond. Each time, the answer was similar. "You know," they would say, "I think it could be nice to be asked. It would be kind of romantic." For a few seconds, the room would be silent. Sometimes I would let them know that I had heard the same response before from students at other schools. As I glanced around the room, I always saw that the answer struck a chord. Students who had previously been very assertive on the topic seemed perplexed, as though their accustomed thought processes were disrupted. They had initially dismissed the idea of asking directly for a kiss, yet one of their peers—perhaps someone they'd have liked to kiss—was telling them that it might work.

On some occasions, we discussed why asking for a kiss is romantic and fun. At other times, we talked about how they could practically frame the question. Could it be, we explored, as simple as, "Can I kiss you?" Usually, that took up all the available time, yet it was enough. I felt that in this particular context, my work was done. The seed for a candid, respectful conversation about consent had been planted. Looking back, what I appreciate the most about these interactions is the extra layer of vulnerability and learning that emerged for many of the students on talk show days. I felt that we touched on questions that truly mattered to many of them. As evidenced by the high levels of engagement and enthusiasm for these special conversations, they gained information and insights with the potential to shape important relationship choices in their futures. These talk shows provided a way into their deepest concerns and curiosities, a chance to share in a **vital conversation.**

VITAL CONVERSATIONS IN MALAWI

Fast-forward a decade and shift the locale halfway around the world to Malawi. I'm sitting in a small room on the shore of Lake Chintheche, with four adolescent boys—street children—from the city of Mzuzu. I'm there in the role of consultant to Children in the Wilderness (CITW), which at the time was creating camp and out-of-school programming for some of the most vulnerable children in Malawi. CITW was dedicated to addressing issues of environmental preservation, employment, education, and HIV prevention.

On this occasion, we were talking about HIV and pregnancy. To create a safer environment for the campers to ask questions, we had decided to separate the boys and girls for this conversation. I was with the boys in one of the dorm rooms, the most private space we could find. The topic of the day was condoms—specifically, the truths, myths, and mechanics of getting them on and off safely. With patient and skillful translation from a Malawian member of staff, we talked through every step. The boys sat facing each other on the edges of two beds, hunched forward, elbows on knees. Their eyes darted back and forth between myself, holding a condom and a banana, and the interpreter.

I opened the floor for questions, which arrived heavy and fast. "What should I do with the condom after I use it?" "Where should I get them?" "Does it feel different with a condom on?" One of the boys locked eyes with me. Then he hesitated and looked down at his feet. I maintained my gaze, so that when he looked up, his eyes met mine. "What do you do if you're with a girl and she wants to have sex with you and you want to have sex with her, but you don't have a condom?" he asked.

This is an incredibly important question. Even with all the facts we had shared about how to use condoms and their effectiveness in preventing pregnancy, HIV, and other sexually transmitted diseases, the question this boy asked spoke to a crucial layer of the conversation. He gave voice to the reality that sometimes it's very difficult to do the right thing.

In that moment, there was one answer I wanted to give, the answer that most sex educators would try to offer. I wanted to tell the boy that no matter how attracted he was to someone, or how much he wanted to have sex, he shouldn't do it without a condom. The risks were so high and the evidence of the risks so compelling that it was a simple choice: don't have sex without a condom.

There was only one problem. If he had felt that the facts spoke for themselves, he wouldn't have asked the question. In his mind, the choice wasn't simple at all. So I asked him, "What's going on for you? Is there another question you're asking?" His response was immediate. "What if you have only one chance with a girl you like a lot, and you really want to have sex with her, and you don't have a condom? It's really hard to walk away."

He had a point. That is a difficult situation, even for many adults. I took a deep breath, then said, "I can't make that decision for you, but I believe that sometimes the person you want to have sex with will respect you more if you have the courage to make sure that sex is safe, for both of you. So if you can tell her that you like her and you want to have sex with her, but you want to wait and get a condom, she might like you more. Sometimes if a person likes you enough to want to have sex with you, they could feel that way again. My guess is you might get a second chance."

This was a difficult answer for me to give. I was worried that I might appear to be failing at my job, which was to educate in a way that would help prevent pregnancy, HIV, and other sexually transmitted illnesses. Yet I also knew that, whatever I said, this boy would make his own choices in situations far from the simple, sanitized reality of the dorm room in which we were sitting. No matter how much I wanted to, I couldn't control the behavior of the boys in that room. I could only hope to support them in making their own choices. When this boy was in the heat of the moment, with someone he was very attracted to, I knew there was a good chance that pregnancy and HIV would feel like abstract concepts. What I wanted was for the conversation to stay with him and for him to make the best decision he could. Telling him to "just say no" to sex was not going to cut it.

WHY IS IT SO HARD TO DO THE SAFE THING?

About three years after that experience, I was outside Cape Town, in Khayelitsha, working with Kwinji and a cadre of her colleagues from Grassroot Soccer. We were running a training course on HIV prevention for twenty to thirty master trainers from all over Africa.

At one point, during a session focused on how young people make choices about sex and condom use, I stopped the discussion and invited the trainers to engage in a brief experiment. I asked them to stand up, close their eyes, and imagine that they were with someone they really liked and they had reached a point where having sex was a real possibility. The only problem was that the condom was in the next room. With their eyes still closed to preserve their anonymity, I asked them to raise their hands if they had been in a similar scenario and decided to go ahead and have unprotected sex. Between a third and a half raised their hands.

After they had lowered their hands and opened their eyes, I confronted the blunt reality of the situation. "You're some of the most knowledgeable sex educators in this part of the world, yet many of us have been in situations we knew were unsafe and carried on anyway. Why is that?"

At first, the room was heavy with silence. "It's hard," one trainer eventually said. "When you're in a room and the lights are off and the sexual energy is flowing, it's very hard to stop and get up to get a condom. The mood could change. What if the other person changes their mind? What if the atmosphere is ruined? So sometimes you just go ahead without the condom."

It was a vulnerable and revealing moment. From a practical perspective, it makes no sense to risk pregnancy and HIV when a condom is a mere fifteen feet away. From a psychological perspective, however, this trainer's answer instantly revealed the layers of complexity that influence these types of decisions. Other people in the room nodded their heads in agreement, and I, too, empathized with his perspective. During the experiment, unbeknownst to the other participants, I was one of those who raised his hand. What followed was a remarkable conversation about the reality of talking with a potential partner about condoms, HIV, pregnancy, and sexuality. It was a conversation that went well beyond facts or statistics, that fostered intense engagement and openness, and that brought the people in that room closer to some of the deepest, most important aspects of the decisions we make about sexuality and relationships.

That was the first time I formally identified the necessity to support vital conversations as a distinct Vital Connection, and we spent a portion of that training working on some of the techniques described in the pages that follow. Looking back, I see that I had been defining and refining this Vital Connection since the days of the talk shows in Maine.

WHAT IS A VITAL CONVERSATION?

As discussed in the introduction, the term *vital conver-*

sation may appear confusingly close to the name for the overall framework of Vital Connections. It's not for lack of effort to come up with a different title. However, I've yet to find a better title to describe these conversations. Vital conversations are at the heart of Vital Connections. They can be difficult, intense, and complicated. However, at their core, they are fundamentally "vital," because they have tremendous potential to have an impact on young people. Often, they reflect the most important needs—both expressed and unexpressed—of the young people in our lives.

A vital conversation is a dialogue that can have a powerful impact on what a person believes or chooses to do. It's a conversation that has the potential to influence a young person's attitude, actions, and well-being. In the example above, there was a surface-level conversation, about the reasons why wearing a condom is a good idea, and then a deeper conversation, about why it's sometimes difficult to follow that advice. By engaging with both the first conversation and the second, an opportunity surfaced to have a more significant influence on a crucial life choice.

Vital conversations are part of a continuum of ways in which we talk with young people. At one end, we engage in **small talk,** which is simple, surface-level conversation. It's usually light and aimed at exchanging minor details of our lives. It fills small chunks of time and keeps people connected. Next is **real talk**. This involves topics that are more meaningful. When we get into real talk, we start to move past facts and explore more of the full picture of who we are, both to ourselves and to others. We tell stories, share experiences, and compare perspectives. Real talk is where relationships begin to take shape. At the other end of the continuum are **vital conversations**. When we get involved in a vital conversation, we're deeply invested in one another. We care about the well-being of the other person. We address the whole person and their context. Vital conversations can change us.

There are five different types of vital conversations I've uncovered and developed over the years. What they all have in common is that they require us to look beyond what young people should or should not be doing and to investigate their deeper experiences, so that they feel their unique story and truth is being honored. This is why supporting vital conversations comes after making time at the right time, knowing their story, and believing they can succeed.

Adopting this approach in certain conversations gives you a greater chance of connecting with young people in a way that they will remember when they have important choices to make. It's easy to tell young people that they don't have enough experience to make sense of the world, or that they're too young to know what they're doing. This creates barriers between adults and young people, diminishing their sense of their own experiences as valuable. Yet that experience is their primary source of information when they're confronted with important decisions. A playground disagreement with a friend or sibling, a breakup with a first crush, an offer to drink alcohol, or the potential to cheat on a test all merit serious care and attention. They are important parts of the choice landscape that young people face, and they come with real consequences.

In workshops, I often invite people to identify and talk about a conversation that has changed them. What I've discovered from this exercise is that everyone can name at least one, and often many. Conversations shape and change lives. When we allow ourselves to engage in vital conversations, we increase our chances of having influence. Facts and rules are important, but the right conversation, at the right time, can have even greater impact.

When a vital conversation concludes, we feel that we've shared something that truly matters. This doesn't always mean that we know exactly what effect we have had or that we can guarantee a young person will make the decision we wish, but we know that we've engaged fully and done everything we can. I don't know whether the young men I spoke to in Malawi always chose to use condoms, or whether all the students I worked with in Maine asked for a kiss, but I know that I did everything I could to meet them where they were and speak with them about their *real* concerns.

PUTTING IT INTO PRACTICE: SUPPORTING VITAL CONVERSATIONS

It's difficult to formally initiate a vital conversation. It *is* possible, however, to be on the lookout for them and support them when they occur. When you apply the other Vital Connections described in this book, you will find that young people become more comfortable and open with you. The job of a skilled youth worker is to listen and understand the signals young people may be sending. It's important to remember that for a vital conversation to be effective, it needs to stem from their needs, not yours.

Our job as youth workers is to do what we can to create an environment in which young people feel safe around us. Part of this involves patiently enduring the tests they may put us through to determine whether we are genuinely trustworthy and interested in them. Our reward will be the kinds of conversations in which young people share parts of their lives that most people, especially adults, may rarely see.

Vital conversations often appear quietly and subtly. As adults, it's a necessity to develop your ability to **listen for conversational clues**. Often, a young person with a topic weighing on their mind will drop a clue to determine whether you're the right person to talk to. The clue may come in words such as, "Sorry I'm late this week. We just had to move in with my grandma." Or it could be found in actions that can be as subtle as lingering for a few minutes after a program is over, just as those girls did with Kwinji in Zimbabwe. These clues are an indication that a young person may wish to share something deeper.

One of the best ways to create the environment for a vital conversation to emerge is simply to **let young people lead the conversations**. Many adults think that they need to shape the flow of the conversations they have with young people. It is a special gift to allow them to express themselves, playing a minor role in the dialogue. You may be surprised by the depth and importance of their talk when they cease to pay attention to your presence and can feel wholly in charge of where the conversation goes.

A third technique is to **be aware of what you wish to talk about with them**. When you find yourself becoming curious about a specific aspect of their story or context, it may be a clue to what the young person in your care most needs to discuss. As a caring adult, you've probably already had the experience of observing a young person and noticing the way they operate. Those observations may have led you to want to explore more aspects of their behavior. For example, maybe you've watched them playing baseball and seen them get into arguments easily. You wish you could talk to them about their anger and the actions it provokes. Perhaps you see them hanging out with a new group of friends and changing how they dress and behave. You realize that they've stopped talking to someone whom they used to be friends with. When you start to notice topics you'd like to broach, you'll be ready to discuss those subjects when young people are ready to talk to you.

FIVE TYPES OF VITAL CONVERSATION

To date, I've identified five types of vital conversations. There are surely more, but these are the ones I've studied the most, both in terms of technique and impact. While you may find yourself engaged in some combination of these five vital conversations, each one has important unique attributes, and each has the potential to make its own difference in a young person's life.

The Sensitive History Conversation

The first type of vital conversation is **sensitive history**. It includes any parts of a young person's story that they wish to share with you. The goal of this conversation is to listen, learn, and glean insight into their vulnerabilities, challenges, aspirations, and context. A sensitive history conversation needn't lead to a specific action. There's usually no decision to be made or problem to solve. The impact comes primarily from a young person sharing their story with a safe, sensitive, and caring adult, who does not criticize their life or choices. I can't overstate how meaningful an outcome it is for some young people simply to have an adult bear witness to a sensitive chapter of their story without judgment.

The need for this conversation may not be immediately obvious. Perhaps a young person arrives late to your program and you ask them why. He shares that he previously missed two weeks of classes at school, and he's now being held after the end of the school day to make up the work. Your first reaction to this revelation might be annoyance at his tardiness. If you approach the situation with curiosity, however, you may wonder what happened to cause him to miss two weeks of school.

The answer could be anything from a simple change of living arrangement to a major family upheaval or tragedy. If you pay attention to the clue—the young person freely sharing the context of their tardiness—you'll be ready to inquire further. If you ask thoughtful follow-up questions, you may gain a whole new understanding of what the young person is going through and needs.

It's quite common for young people to share small pieces of their stories in hopes that adults will show an interest and ask further questions or to test whether they find the adult trustworthy. Many of us fail those tests. We're afraid of asking, or we don't have time. Perhaps we're not even listening. When you want to encourage a young person to continue sharing, you can simply invite them to tell you more. You can validate their experience, letting them know that you appreciate their giving you access to a piece of their story. The purpose of the sensitive history conversation is not to pry into a young person's life but to create a space for them to share what they need to share with you. You will be surprised how often a sensitive history conversation serves as the gateway to other vital conversations.

Some young people need to talk about how difficult it is to find a quiet place to study, or share that there are six children in their home and they feel like they don't get enough attention. Others may need to confide in an adult about even more serious issues. There are parts of everyone's story that reveal important details about who they are, why they do what they do, and what they need. It's our responsibility to be on the lookout for the times that a young person wants to tell us more of their story.

The Reframing Conversation

The second type of vital conversation is **reframing**. This involves seeing a young person's experience from a new perspective and helping them look at themselves from a different angle. The objectives of a reframing conversation are to understand how a young person understands themselves and, simultaneously, to reinforce positive perspectives and counter negative self-perceptions.

When young people feel that their sense of self-efficacy is under threat or experience certain failures, they may experience it as a catastrophe and generalize it as a deficit in their identity or character. Too quickly and too often, their conclusion is, "X happened, so I must be a bad kid." As caring adults, we can insert ourselves into their internal dialogues and represent an alternative voice. We need to interrupt their demeaning self-talk and provide them with new information and new lenses through which to see both the situation and themselves.

To be clear, I am *not* suggesting that you try to gloss over bad experiences. The reframing conversation is about helping young people see a more balanced picture of their outlook and abilities, and resist the dangerous spiral into self-doubt. Reframing is an act of stepping back from a situation and putting it into a different perspective. You do this by giving young people your honest version of events. I've seen many poignant examples of youth workers engaging with young people in an attempt to reframe the way they were seeing a situation. Yet one of the best examples I've encountered recently occurred during the finals of a national sports tournament.

In the United States, men's college basketball is one of the most popular spectator sports, especially during the national tournament known as March Madness. In 2017, the University of Oregon reached the Final Four of the tournament and was matched against the University of North Carolina (UNC). With only a few seconds to play, Oregon was down by four points. One of the Oregon players strategically fouled a UNC player in hopes that he would miss at least one of his free throws. He missed both; however, Oregon failed to collect the rebound and launch a counterattack. So they immediately committed another strategic foul. Again, the UNC player missed both free throws. And again, Oregon could not pull down the rebound they desperately needed. A few seconds later, the buzzer sounded and the game was over. UNC moved on to the national championships, while Oregon was eliminated.

Statistically, Oregon was a better rebounding team than UNC. They had their best rebounder positioned directly under the hoop. Yet he could not grab the crucial rebound. After the game ended, the story surfaced that there had been a delay in allowing reporters into Oregon's locker room. Their top rebounder was so distraught that the coach barred anyone from coming into the locker room until the player could be consoled. The young man was devastated. He felt he had lost the game for his team.

Probably, only the coach, the player, and the rest of the

Oregon team know what was said behind those closed locker room doors. Nonetheless, it's a credit to that coach that he created a small buffer of time to help the player make sense of what had happened. Had I been in the coach's position, I might have reminded the player of the great game he played, showing him the stats to prove it. I might have described the numerous other missed opportunities his teammates had to change the outcome of the game. I might have offered a different perspective on what I thought about him as a player and his performance, giving him the chance to perceive his efforts differently.

Crucially, reframing is not an attempt to erase a young person's feelings of hurt or disappointment. When we enter a reframing conversation, we are seeking to offer an alternative perspective on a difficult experience. There's a fine line between helping someone reframe their experience and telling them something they don't want to hear, and it often takes some time for a different narrative to permeate a young person's psyche.

I find that it helps to use the phrase, "Let me tell you what I see." This phrase allows you to share your experience in a way that presents your perspective as an option to consider, not as a criticism. You may want to say, "I'm going to respectfully disagree with your view of the situation." Alternatively, you can ask, "What evidence do you have to support what you're saying?" This allows you to counter with evidence of a different story. A confidence-shaking loss can be a moment when a young person finds evidence that makes them think they are a loser. Alternatively, it can be a learning moment, one of a hundred opportunities to build strength and resilience.

This kind of conversation calls for a little more assertiveness than a sensitive history conversation. It requires you to actively present a fresh perspective. There's no need to sugarcoat a situation and lie to someone who has truly played a bad game or failed a test. The reframing conversation is about rewriting a negative story based on palpable evidence, not rewriting history. Sometimes I've heard reframing statements such as, "You're not stupid; you're amazing." While this is well intentioned, it's not particularly helpful. It's not a new story; it's only vague praise. Reframing is specific and evidence-based.

Ultimately, like each of the five vital conversations, you can't control whether your efforts hit the mark. You can only offer a young person your perspective and hope that they internalize your story. Perhaps after weighing the evidence, they may start to feel differently about themselves.

The Problem-Solving Conversation

The third type of vital conversation is **problem solving**. The goal of this conversation is to generate options, explore the complexities and nuances of a life challenge, and nurture healthy decision making. It's an opportunity for a young person to reveal how they make decisions and for us to share some of the ways *we* make decisions.

Young people face a host of challenges and choices, many of which are significant and consequential. Some are beyond their power to control or manage, but others present opportunities to grow, learn, and test their critical thinking. When we find ourselves inside a problem-solving conversation with a young person, we have the chance to influence one of the most important aspects of life: making decisions.

Supporting a problem-solving conversation starts with one important disclaimer: Don't offer unsolicited advice, even if you're certain you know the best course of action. You may have faced a similar problem in your life, but your goal is to support the agency of that young person, not tell them what to do. The power of this conversation is that it is truly a dialogue. Telling a young person what to do, unless they've specifically requested your advice, is a surefire way to derail or shut down a promising exchange.

Generally speaking, we do a decent job of teaching facts and dispensing knowledge to young people. To some degree, we also provide them with useful techniques they need to engage in critical thinking. However, I think we've yet to crack the code on equipping young people with a full set of tools to solve practical problems in their lives, particularly when it comes to making important health-seeking decisions.

In almost every intervention I'm part of, I challenge the program leadership and staff to create space in their activities schedule for what we call Team Time. Team Time is a simple yet remarkably powerful exercise. It's a few minutes at the end of each program session during which a group of participants sit together, processing their experiences of the day. I've seen it serve as the perfect backdrop for all five of the vital conversations to take shape, especially the one involving problem solving.

On one occasion, while observing the E2F program in Gaza, I had the chance to watch one of our staff lead Team Time. Her name was Reem. She demonstrated many of the skills I've been describing in this book, bringing them all to bear during a ten-minute Team Time discussion with a small group of nine- to twelve-year-old Palestinian children. Having worked with the group for several months, Reem had already developed a strong rapport with the children. She cared deeply for each of them, and they trusted her.

She started by asking what they enjoyed about the day's activities. A lively conversation ensued. Then she shifted the tone of the conversation, asking, "Is there anything that frightens you?" These children lived in Gaza, arguably one of the more dangerous places in the world. With a near-constant risk of bombs falling in their communities, these children had many reasons to be frightened. Reem, however, resisted the temptation to direct the conversation based on any assumptions. She simply asked the question and waited. At first, everyone was silent. A few children looked down at the ground. Some swung their feet back and forth under the plastic chairs where they were seated. They were thinking.

Finally, one girl raised her hand. Reem acknowledged her with a nod. The girl said, "What's really hard for me is that I get scared walking home from school sometimes."

Reem asked her why.

"The streets change. A road gets closed for construction or a building is bombed. One day, it's fine to walk down a street, but the next day, I have to find a different way home."

Some communities in Gaza are densely populated and the roads can be mazelike in their complexity. It was easy to see how a nine-year-old might become confused by all the changes to road layouts. Reem continued to listen attentively. Sure enough, one of the boys raised his hand

and said, "Me, too. Sometimes I don't know where I'm supposed to go."

Before long, other children chimed in, contributing to a poignant conversation about how hard it was to find their way home. You might imagine that bigger fears would have occupied their minds, but on this specific day, they were worried about finding their way home. Reem listened, asked a few questions about how they could solve this problem, and by the end of Team Time, they created a plan to help one another get home safely from school. They decided to walk home together and remind one another of the right streets. Reem never told the children what to do. She didn't instruct them. She simply supported this vital problem-solving conversation.

Underlying the problem-solving conversation are two important premises. First, young people have tremendous abilities to solve their own problems, and they benefit from having many opportunities to practice solving difficult real-life challenges. Second, we almost always have more than one option, and one of the best ways to come up with effective solutions is to enlist more people in the search. Too often in life, especially when we experience distress, our thinking narrows. We see only a few possibilities. The problem-solving conversation can help young people to evaluate their options in a safe, calm environment, assisting them in building a practical skill set they can apply to future challenges.

There are several questions you can use when you're engaging in problem-solving conversations. "What's the problem you're trying to solve here?" "What's most important to you, and why?" "Do you know how to solve this?" "Would you like to hear how I might solve this?" Those questions can lead to suggestions such as, "Let's come up with some more options," or "Let's make a list." Not a week of a young person's life goes by when they're not trying to solve some important problem. As a caring adult, you may be able to help the young people in your life reach health-seeking decisions and hone their problem-solving skills, all while supporting their autonomy and the choices they make.

The Feedback Conversation

The fourth type of vital conversation is **feedback**. Feedback typically takes the form of appreciation or critique, and its intention is usually to improve or reinforce some aspect of a person's behavior or performance. For many people, it's challenging to deliver effective feedback, especially to young people. Young people can only make use of feedback if they trust that it's delivered with skill and respect. If they're not open to it, it's unlikely that they will receive it positively and act on it.

There are several ways into the feedback conversation. You can say, "I'd like to share what I observe about you," or "I'd like to talk about the impact of your actions and find out whether those are the results you want." You might ask directly, "Can I offer you some feedback?" or "Do you want to try something different next time?" You'll probably find that the most effective way to frame the conversation is to make it clear to the young person you're talking to that you want to help and to give feedback that is rich with detail and evidence.

Having delivered it, it's important to give them a chance first to react and then to respond. The reaction comes first, and you can expect that it may have an emotional element. The young person may be surprised, frustrated, excited, or confused. Give them a few minutes to process your feedback.

Even when feedback is given well, it can still be hard to hear. It's usually wise to follow up with a second conversation to gauge the young person's response, otherwise their actual response and the opportunity to help them make use of your feedback may be swallowed up in their reaction. To frame this, you can say, "This may be a lot for you to hear. It should probably be two conversations, so let me offer you feedback today. We can talk about how you feel about it. Then take some time and think about it. Let's plan to talk again tomorrow. We can follow up, and you can ask questions."

Here's an example. Picture a girl who's been disrupting an activity. You might say, "I've noticed that you're having a hard time with this activity, and it seems that some of your peers are distracted by your behavior. Can I give you feedback on what I see and what you could do to make the situation better?"

If she agrees to receive your feedback, you can continue: "It seems that when you sit with your friends, you find it hard to focus. I wonder whether you want to think about moving to a different seat. I know that when you sit in the front, you tend to pay more attention." By providing a specific example and suggesting a solution, you invite her to consider her own behavior and determine whether another strategy would serve her better.

Besides aiding in the development of young people, the feedback conversation serves an additional crucial purpose. One of the most important skills for a young person to possess, especially as they transition into adulthood, is coachability. Coachability is the power to receive feedback, whether it's recognition or critique, absorb the key messages and opportunities for improvement, and apply it to future actions and thinking. Coachability is an essential skill for succeeding at work and in relationships. By engaging in feedback conversations with young people, we can help them hone this essential life skill.

The Bottom-Story Conversation

The final type of vital conversation is the **bottom story**. This type of conversation is about exploring beneath the surface. The goal of the bottom-story conversation is to uncover parts of a topic or issue that are sensitive, difficult to talk about, or nuanced. These are not easy conversations to navigate. Yet in my experience, the bottom-story conversation has the greatest potential to make a major impact on the life of a young person.

We all know the "shoulds" of life, yet few of us live every day according to them. We should regularly eat healthy food in moderate portions. We should avoid smoking. We should study hard and stay in school. We should steer clear of drugs. We should use a condom. Life is complicated, and often these "shoulds" are insufficient to fully guide our behavior. The goal of the bottom-story conversation is to acknowledge that sometimes life is not as clean or easy as we'd like it to be. If we can discover what lies beneath the surface, we may be able to navigate these situations more safely and effectively.

As the name of this conversation implies, some conversations comprise both a top story and a bottom story. The top story includes all the information we have easy access to, along with the expectations society places on us to act on that information. It is generally the black-and-white, good-and-bad, right-and-wrong layer of the conversation.

The bottom story is everything else—in other words, the gray areas. It's the complicated emotions, the unique context, and personal needs and pressures that shape our actual choices. This bottom-story conversation combines elements of all the other types of vital conversation. It requires a level of confidence and comfort with sensitive topics. The topics that emerge in a bottom-story conversation may be difficult to sit with, triggering a desire to control the young person's behavior and push away the reality of their experience. Yet it's especially important to avoid telling young people what to do during bottom-story conversations. These are conversations of trust.

To spark a bottom-story conversation, you may ask, "Is there something you want to talk about, but you're embarrassed or afraid to discuss?" or "What's going on for you beneath the surface of this topic?" You can say, "What are we not talking about here that might help you?" or "Can we talk about why it's hard to do the thing you're expected to do?" It's essential to remain nonjudgmental in these conversations, to give young people the space they need to say the things they're afraid to say.

As described at the beginning of this chapter, one of my favorite ways to invite young people to open up and access deeper stories is to run a talk show. While I first experienced the power of the talk show format in Maine during the mid-nineties, I received a potent reminder a decade later, when I was in Malawi working with an HIV/AIDS teen club run by Baylor Hospital. In this setting, I used the talk show format as a way of getting at bottom-story conversations with a group of about fifty HIV-positive teenagers.

The topic of the show was disclosure of one's HIV-positive status. At the time, and even today for many people, disclosing HIV status is a risky decision. There's a stigma attached to being HIV-positive, which can translate into a real chance that a person acknowledging their HIV status could be subject to discrimination, isolation, or even physical harm from friends, family, and the wider community. At the same time, living with HIV without a support network is very difficult, so disclosing to the right people has real benefits. A young person who discloses their HIV status to the right people can receive more of the support they need. This is all part of the top story.

We wanted the teens to hear these messages and, ideally, to consider disclosing their status to people who would protect and support them. We also knew, however, that some young people in the audience would need a deeper conversation about whom to disclose to and how to decide whom to trust.

As the talk show progressed, we began to explore deeper aspects of disclosure. Members of the audience shared some of their fears, explaining what was at stake for them if they disclosed their status to the wrong person. We didn't pass judgment on any of their concerns. Instead, we acknowledged the real risks and challenges, and the reasons why people might choose not to disclose to anyone.

On the floor, against the side wall, sat a boy, probably thirteen or fourteen years old. A small entourage of friends surrounded him. From my vantage point in the room, he had appeared disengaged from the activity, but I've learned from experience that young people who appear uninterested are often paying close attention. The conversation continued for another twenty minutes until, unexpectedly, he raised his hand.

"I have an answer. Here's what I do. I pick a secret, but not my HIV status. Maybe there's a girl I like. I tell someone I think I can trust and ask them not to tell anyone else. Then I wait about two weeks to find out whether my secret comes out. If the secret gets out, I know I can't trust that friend; but if the secret doesn't get out, I know I can trust them. Maybe then I'll tell them my HIV status."

I doubt that any adult in that room could have come up with such an elegant and brilliant solution. I'm sure that every teenager in the room was making mental notes. I'm equally certain that this boy would not have joined the conversation if not for the atmosphere in the room and the willingness of all the adults to engage in dialogue at both the top- and the bottom-story levels of this vital conversation.

VITAL CONVERSATIONS NEED YOU

Sherry Turkle is a social scientist and professor at MIT. In her book *Reclaiming Conversation*, she writes that "A child alone with a problem has an emergency, a child in conversation with an adult and facing a problem is learning how to cope with it."[8] When we enter fully into the realities of young people's lives and explore their experiences with them through genuine, respectful, and candid conversations, so much becomes possible. It's a dynamic that constantly renews, as one vital conversation opens up the space in which another can take place.

As with every other Vital Connection described in this book, opportunities to access and support vital conversations exist all around us. When we make time at the right time, get to know the stories of the young people in our lives, and believe they can succeed, we may soon discover that vital conversations are ready to burst out of them. Then powerful and beautiful things can happen. There are very few young people in the world who wouldn't benefit from the right conversation at the right time.

---

8   Sherry Turkle, *Reclaiming Conversation: The Power of Talk in a Digital Age* (New York: Penguin, 2015).

Conversation connects. Conversation teaches. Conversation heals.

The final two chapters of this book are shorter than the preceding two, but no less important. They center on a discussion about Vital Connections that takes you outside the standard realm of youth workers. They involve actions that may require you to think differently about your role and go further than you thought you could or should in support of young people. They're not for everyone, and that's OK, but they have the potential to make an equally and sometimes more profound difference in the lives of young people.

PART THREE

COMMUNITY AND COMMITMENT

CHAPTER FIVE

FACILITATE CONNECTIONS WITH OTHER CARING ADULTS

* * * * * * *

The drive from Windhoek, the capital of Namibia, out to the Namib-Naukluft National Park takes about six hours. The last third takes place on dusty gravel roads that wreak havoc on any vehicle other than a four-wheel-drive truck. We were traveling in minivans that seated a maximum of twelve people. Each of our two vans carried three to four adults and twelve to fifteen campers. The air-conditioning couldn't cool us all, so we rocked and dozed, side to side, sweating and breathing the warm air. Namibia's weather is hot all year, and in December it was reaching between 100 and 110 degrees Fahrenheit—sometimes even hotter— during mid-afternoon.

It was December 2002, and we were transporting a group

of first-time campers from the SOS Children's Village outside Windhoek to the Kulala Tented Camp, where we were launching Namibia's first season of Children in the Wilderness (CITW). First-time camps are always beset with both anticipated and unforeseen challenges. I've come to trust that while they never go the way I expect, with the right staff, first-time camps almost always turn out great. I didn't know it yet, but we had the right staff.

During the drive, however, I had my doubts. Our camp leadership team consisted of three safari guides, all employed by the project's parent company, Wilderness Safaris, and myself. The guides had no formal youth work experience. We were piloting a weeklong residential camp program at an untested site, with extremely limited facilities—five platform tents, a small open-air lodge, and a plunge pool, all surrounded by approximately nineteen thousand square miles of harsh desert wilderness.

Yet there were signs that things would work. The logistics and planning for the camp were impeccable. I should have expected nothing less from safari guides accustomed to working with demanding tourists, tracking game in the bush, and planning and leading detailed itineraries. The food, the water (which was trucked in), the schedule, and the materials were all meticulously organized and prepared. In addition, my primary collaborator, Ben Forbes, one of the three guides, had worked hard to form a strong relationship with SOS and had immersed himself in the details to ensure that the children were prepared for their adventure.

As we bumped along down the dirt road, every sleepy head and body swaying in unison with each turn of the van, my mind was preoccupied with one lingering issue: our team of counselors. SOS is an international organization that works with orphans. They selected each one of our campers. The counselors also came from SOS. Before we met them, I was told they would be between eighteen and twenty years old. A week earlier, however, as we had arrived to collect them for their counselor training, I was instantly struck by how small they looked. As we approached, I contemplated the impact of malnutrition and early childhood deprivation on physical development. When I stepped out of the vehicle and looked more closely, however, I realized that they were healthy and vibrant—for fourteen- and fifteen-year-olds!

Somewhere in the back-and-forth between Ben and the director of the Children's Village, confusion arose between the expected age of the counselors and which children at the orphanage were the "oldest." Less than a week before launch, we found ourselves with a group of counselors who were barely teenagers, preparing to facilitate a camp population aged between nine and fourteen. It was an unexpected scenario, but we made it work.

From the first time we met our counselors, one stood out. His name was Franco Morao. First, he was a head taller than any of the others. Second, he exuded a quiet confidence that spoke of maturity and wisdom. Finally, as soon as camp began, it became obvious that he was ideally suited to working with children. It helped that he knew all the campers, because they lived together throughout the year. More than this, he had an intuitive understanding of both camp and group leadership. We ran that camp for three weeks, and Franco became more and more of a star.

From its inception, the camp had several objectives. One was an environmental protection mission, hoping to inform and inspire. Another was instilling key life skills related to decision making and risk taking. A third goal was creating an employment pathway for Namibian children to work in the ecotourism sector. In the inaugural year of the camp, we talked about someday inviting "graduates" to use their camp certificate as a ticket to a job interview with the camp's parent safari company.

Franco did just that. He returned to camp, season after season, becoming one of the most talented camp counselors I have ever worked with. When he turned eighteen, he applied for employment with Wilderness Safaris. They hired him. Soon, he joined the guide-training program. Within a few years, he was working full time as a guide, supporting himself and his siblings.

BUILDING A SUPPORT SYSTEM OF CARING ADULTS

In the years I worked with Franco, I hope that I taught him a few things about youth work. At the very least, he picked up some songs, games, and a handful of camp characters from me. But I wasn't the caring adult he needed the most. It was Ben, and Sunday, and Lloyd, and the other staff from Wilderness Safaris with whom Franco connected most deeply. While he tended to his campers on desert hikes, he also watched Ben, Sunday, and Lloyd guide. Around the campfire, he listened closely to their career stories.

I don't know exactly when the spark caught for Franco. We certainly weren't equipped to formally recruit him during those first weeks of camp, nor did we intentionally match him with a particular staff member. What matters is he found the right adults to connect with, and they opened the door for him to pursue a career path he might otherwise never have considered. Like so many of the stories in this book, I didn't absorb the full meaning of Franco's until years later. As I reflect on it now, I think about the circumstances that brought him and these safari guides together. What I've come to realize is that it is less important for every young person I work with to connect to me than it is for them to find the adults *they* need to connect to.

Until now, we've been exploring what you can say and do in your interactions with young people to have the greatest possible impact on their lives. In this chapter, we take a step back from direct interactions and conversations to acknowledge an important truth: It's not realistic or feasible for one adult to be everything to a young person. Sometimes, the most important thing you can do for a young person is to search your network and beyond and become a bridge to someone else. The fifth Vital Connection is **facilitating connections with other caring adults.**

Connecting a young person to other caring adults isn't an indication of weakness or lack of effort or skill on your part. No single adult—not even a parent—can or should be the sole source of support to any given young person. To thrive, and in many cases even to survive, a young person needs a network of caring adults, who play various roles at various times. Each young person needs teachers, coaches, doctors, mentors, caregivers, role models, and many more. This web of adults, each bringing something different, creates a support system that can dramatically increase the odds of a young person navigating challenges, capitalizing on opportunities, and reaching their aspirations.

It is a well-known expression that "it takes a village to raise a child." The effort, empathy, and commitment required to support a young person on their journey to adulthood is tremendous. Facilitating connections to other caring adults is not a last resort to turn to when you've exhausted your time, energy, and ideas. By then, it might be too late to help effectively. It is one of the six Vital Connections for a reason. It is a core part of the repertoire of the most effective caring adults.

When a young person like Franco connects with the right caring adults, he experiences two benefits. First, he is more likely to get his needs met. Second, he comes to see that more than one adult cares about him.

Knowing that they matter to more than one adult may seem like a small success, but it is significant. For a young person in need, they have one more person to call upon. If self-doubt or self-criticism starts to creep into their mind, they have one more positive voice to challenge those distressing internal monologues.

You, too, will benefit from facilitating connections with other caring adults. First, you're relieved of some of the pressure that comes with trying to meet the complicated needs of a young person on your own, especially if some of those needs lie outside of your skillset or beyond your resources. Second, you gain your own support system of other caring adults. Finally, you increase the odds of achieving your fundamental objective: helping a young person you care about reach their goals.

I love hearing about and learning from some of the many organizations that are working actively to create the "villages" of caring adults young people need. A few years ago, I visited an urban running program in Philadelphia called Students Run Philly Style (SRPS). This organization has built an after-school running club that helps young people train for long-distance races, particularly half and full marathons. Philadelphia has a large and vibrant running community, and SRPS has succeeded in engaging many local adult volunteers in their program.

During warm-ups, training runs, and cooldown time, adult volunteers are encouraged to spread themselves out, maximizing the potential for connection between runners and volunteers. This kind of intentional mixing facilitates ample opportunities for the participants to form connections with many different caring adults in the program. On my visit, one of the program directors shared a story about where one of these connections led. A participant was on a run with an adult volunteer. Their route took them through a part of downtown Philadelphia that the young person had never visited, and he was amazed by the height of the buildings. The volunteer happened to work in one of the buildings and gave the young person a tour. By the time the tour was complete, the volunteer had offered the young runner an internship working with him in that building.

Another sport program serving homeless populations, Street Soccer USA (SSUSA), uses a similar approach. SSUSA integrates numerous volunteer coaches and staff into their training sessions and actively encourages each participant to form multiple connections. In some of the SSUSA city programs, they enter teams into corporate leagues, competing for the entire season against teams of non-homeless players. During warm-ups and post-game interactions, the SSUSA players get crucial opportunities to build their networks, extending them well beyond the volunteer coaching staff. In cities where SSUSA manages their own fields, they run their own corporate leagues, planning barbecues and other events to bring their players into regular interaction with the rest of the players in the league.

What both of these organizations have in common is the belief that more adults are better than fewer adults. Further, they train and prepare staff to engage directly with their target population. They strike a balance between formal and informal time so that interactions can lead to meaningful connections. And they often make it an explicit goal of their program to promote networking and connections among all those participating.

In Baltimore, an exceptional organization called Thread has the goal of supporting underperforming high school students. Thread's approach is grounded in facilitating connections between each young person and a "family" of caring adults. The program requires a major commitment. Each student in the program is matched with up to five volunteers who commit themselves to doing whatever it takes to support that student for up to a decade. The organization then layers in additional "threads" of other adults who can contribute what a particular student needs, thus creating a near-indestructible web of support. The results are incredible: The vast majority—more than 80 percent—of students who have been part of the program for five years or more graduate from high school and are accepted into college.[9]

In spring 2017, a colleague from Edgework, Maren Rojas, and I were working with Legacy Youth Tennis and Education in Philadelphia, delivering a two-day Vital Connections workshop. Well into the second day of training, one of the veteran coaches shared this story.

Each day, during tennis practice, they provided a simple snack for the players, typically a banana. The standard allocation was one banana per player, but this coach noticed that one of the girls was taking two, three, or even four. After observing this for several days, he sat with her to inquire what was going on. She revealed that her mother was working additional shifts in the evenings

---

9   Thread, "The Success," https://www.thread.org/what-we-do/ (retrieved December 20, 2017).

and that her older brother was coming home from school during the day to sneak food from the house. By the time this girl and her younger siblings came home from school, there was very little food left to eat. They couldn't afford more food, and her mother was reluctant to reprimand her son because she feared he would turn to more dangerous behaviors to feed himself.

The coach knew he couldn't change this girl's circumstances or provide her family with enough food. However, with a simple call, he was able to connect her with a colleague affiliated with a school lunch program that provided her with access to more food during the school day.

Last, there is one specific important connection to another adult I want to highlight, one that is required by law: mandated reporting. Nowhere does society's collective responsibility to protect children come into sharper relief. Mandated reporting is a legal obligation for many professionals who work with or have regular contact with young people. If they know of situations of neglect or abuse, they must make a report to the local child protection agency. This agency works to assess each situation and has the power to remove children from their living situation if it is judged to be too damaging. The first law requiring mandated reporting was passed in 1963, in response to studies that described what was called the battered child syndrome. In 1975, a comprehensive law was passed to provide protection to children experiencing neglect or abuse.

Today, many adults working in professions that serve young people are mandated reporters. This includes teachers, mental health professionals, health-care providers, and social workers. They are taught to share a specific message when a young person discloses abuse or neglect: "I know this is not easy for you to tell me about. However, if I hear a young person like yourself share with me the kinds of things you are experiencing, it means you are asking for help. And I'm not the person who can help you. But I know who can, and what I can do is help you get connected to the right people."

Admittedly, mandated reporting has its flaws. There is no guarantee that the system that a child is referred to will protect them effectively: there have been tragic cases where the referral has done more harm than good. However, mandated reporting has also saved many children from abusive and traumatizing circumstances.

In the context of Vital Connections, mandated reporting represents a resounding call for connectivity. Every young person needs to hear and internalize the message that *someone* can help. And every youth worker needs to recognize that there are times when they're not the right person to do so. The message a mandated reporter sends to a child is the same message any youth worker sends to a young person in less dire circumstances, who needs a doctor, a tutor, a job referral, or a counselor: "You need something I can't provide. However, I can get you connected to the right caring adult who can help you."

PUTTING IT INTO PRACTICE: FACILITATING CONNECTIONS WITH OTHER CARING ADULTS

Exercising this Vital Connection begins with the belief that more adults are better than fewer adults. One adult is better than none, but two are probably much better than one, especially if the second can give a young person something the first can't. When the number creeps up to three or four, that young person likely has the makings of an all-star support team behind them.

Kathleen Kimball-Baker authored a book in 2005 called, *Connect 5: Finding the Caring Adults You May Not Realize Your Teen Needs.* Each short chapter in the book identifies a different type of adult who could be a benefit to a young person. It's a rich resource and a useful reminder that the number and type of caring adults available to any young person is important.

The act of facilitating quality connections with other caring adults starts with self-reflection. There are four questions you can ask yourself to guide your approach in this area. The first is, **"What does this young person really need?"** Think about where they are struggling, what opportunities they are missing, what their goals are, and what you wish for them to achieve. Think about their future, both short term and long term.

There are at least six important areas of need to consider. The first is **access to services.** This can be anything from psychological counseling to medical care to job placement. The second is **training, teaching, or additional education,** including interview skills and tutoring. The third is **structure and boundaries,** perhaps in the form of a program that brings more predictability to their days, or groups that meet before or after school, or on weekends. Structure may also include an adult who provides transport for the young person to ensure they get to school or their job on time. It is far too easy for a vulnerable young person to slip through the cracks in transit or transition from one activity to the next.

The fourth category is **guidance and perspective** from an adult who has specific experiences or expertise to share. The fifth is **support and empathy,** based on the willingness and ability of some adults to provide pure listening and care. Finally, young people can often benefit a great deal from **connecting with role models,** especially someone who has been where this person is now and with whom the young person can deeply identify. A struggling young person who meets a role model may internalize the message, "She made it. Maybe I can, too." It's important that these role models are close enough in age and experience for young people to identify with them and feel that their accomplishments are within reach.

It's also important to allow this process to be led by the needs of the young person. You may be tempted to think first about *whom* you know, but resist making a connection until you've thought deeply about *what* the young person in question needs. If you aren't sure—and even if you are—consider involving them in the process. Sit down with them and talk openly about your intentions. Invite their responses. You may uncover a hidden need you had not previously considered.

The second question is, **"Which of their needs may be beyond what I can realistically provide or could be provided more effectively by someone else?"** Be honest with yourself. There is a difference between what you want to do for this young person and what you realistically have the time, skill, or resources to provide. It could be that you're limited by your role and it's not appropriate for you to spend time with a young person on the weekend or help them to find a job. Perhaps you don't have time to give them the support they need. Maybe you lack essential knowledge to meet the young person's needs, or they won't allow you to help them in a certain area of their life. When you know the answer to this question, you can make a realistic assessment of the gaps in what you can provide.

The third question is, **"Whom do I know who could meet those needs?"** Within this third question lie three sequenced subquestions. The first subquestion is, **"Who is the optimal type of person to play this role, based on their skills and their motivation?"** The second subquestion is, **"Do I know anyone in my network who fulfills these criteria?"** If yes, then you can move to question four. If not, then the final subquestion is, **"Whom do I know who may know someone like this?"** If you don't know the type of adult you think the young person needs, then you may find yourself in the position of networking on behalf of the young person in your care.

Finally, the fourth question is, **"How can I facilitate the connection?"** First, it's important that both the adult and the young person *want* to meet. Talk to the young person about your intentions and the benefits of the connection, asking them to affirm that they're interested and willing. It's important they understand that you're not ending your connection with them, and that the new connection represents the growth and enrichment of their caring adult network. You may also choose to meet the adult and explain in person why you want to connect them with the young person and why they're a good fit. You can talk about why they're important to you, what their needs are, why it matters to meet those needs, and what you think this other adult can provide.

Once both the adult and the young person are informed and enthusiastic about the connection, make the introduction. It's possible that you'll need to follow up and make sure that a connection has taken place, because introductions don't always work the first time. Sometimes they misfire. If you believe in the potential of the connection, you may need to be present to facilitate the first connection.

Historically, the village served as a central organizing structure for many people. Villages were the location where people found the goods and services they could not produce on their own. The village housed the cobbler, the blacksmith, the school, the doctor, and the bank. Now, picture a slightly different kind of village, one that contains all the adults who could have a positive impact on the life of a young person. You have this unique opportunity to take that young person on a tour of the village and help them discover the power of having an entire team of caring adults on their side.

As you walk the village streets, you can help this young person meet a tutor, coach, mentor, role model, or friend. Franco found his path to becoming a tour guide through his experiences with the CITW "village" of caring adults. These potential villages are all around us, yet it is up to us to activate them for the young people in our care. With each thoughtful connection you facilitate, you amplify your potential for impact and increase the chances of that young person finding what they need.

CHAPTER SIX

INTERVENE WHEN THEY NEED YOU MOST

* * * * * * *

In December 2000, my father and I embarked on a cross-country adventure by train from Boston to San Francisco. Somewhere between Cleveland and Chicago, the trip went figuratively south. We were traveling between Christmas and New Year's and found ourselves caught in an epic snowstorm. Our train fell further and further behind schedule. We left Cleveland eight hours late. Somewhere in western Ohio, the train was hit by an SUV that skidded on the ice at a desolate railroad crossing. After detaching the vehicle from the train, the journey finally restarted, now more than fifteen hours behind schedule, with many more hours of travel until Chicago.

Then the toilets stopped functioning. The café car shut down, and fresh water became scarce. We stopped repeatedly, for no apparent reason, in the middle of nowhere, idled for anywhere from ten to thirty minutes, and then started to move again. Our maximum speed never seemed to exceed thirty miles per hour. At one of these seemingly random stops, in Indiana, a frazzled conductor scurried down the aisle of our car asking if anyone was a doctor. Receiving no response, he quickly disappeared into the next car.

At the time, I was a Massachusetts-licensed emergency medical technician (EMT), with exactly zero hours of time logged working on an ambulance. I had earned the license only a year earlier. When the conductor returned a few minutes later, alone, I hesitantly raised my hand and said, "I'm an EMT." He let out a gasp of relief and said, "Follow me." A few cars up, the conductor directed me to a woman who appeared to be in her seventies. A quick assessment revealed that she was diabetic, had run out of her medication on the train, and appeared to be experiencing the onset of a diabetic emergency, a heart attack, or both.

A retired nurse soon joined me. We did our best to keep her calm, offering her orange juice and a cookie. To the dismay of everyone on the train, we also insisted that the conductor stop the train at the next railroad crossing, no matter where it was, and coordinate with local emergency medical services to transport her to a hospital as fast as possible.

Once we'd agreed on the plan, there was little else to do but wait and do our best to keep the lady calm. So I sat with her, and we started to chat. She was a grandmother. In fact, sitting next to her was her terrified preteen granddaughter. The woman told me that she was in the process of relocating her granddaughter to live with her in Chicago—as far away as possible from the girl's current home in Florida.

Her daughter lived in Florida and had become involved in a relationship that was putting her granddaughter in danger. With her granddaughter sitting within earshot next to us, I didn't inquire about the details, but I got the distinct impression it was a very bad situation. Heartbroken that she couldn't extract her daughter, she had nonetheless worked tirelessly to obtain custody of her granddaughter. The final step was the brutally long round trip from Chicago to Florida. Taxed by the bus journey south, she had made the decision to return north by train.

This woman was sweating, scared, and in pain, yet she shared her story with a deep conviction and authority. She had made up her mind to help her granddaughter, and nothing, not even her own health challenges, was going to stop her. As I leaned over to check her pulse, I stole a glance at her granddaughter. The girl was hunched over, her fingers clasped together tightly on her lap, frozen in silence. I didn't know whether she was shy, traumatized from her experiences in Florida, or petrified that she could lose the one person who had showed up to look out for her.

A few minutes later, the train stopped and a pair of real EMTs climbed into the train car, covered in snow up to their knees. They had trekked across a field to reach the train. While the EMTs escorted the woman and her granddaughter off the train, I wished with all my heart that she would make it to the hospital in time and that both she and her granddaughter would be OK. She had navigated the court system, spent a significant amount of money to create this arrangement, reconfigured her life to prepare to care for her granddaughter, and crossed half the country to protect her. For both their sakes, I hoped that she would survive.

THE PROBLEM WITH BOUNDARIES

Unlike the opening stories for the other five Vital Connections, the above account didn't originate from a youth program context. It's a story I stumbled into of a grandmother trying to take care of her granddaughter, caught up in a treacherous train ride in a snowstorm. As you read about this sixth and final Vital Connection, you'll discover that it is very different from the other five. It's unbounded. It blurs professional and personal lines. It's also one of the truest expressions of commitment and unconditional love.

Throughout my life, I have heard stories from many people in my personal and professional circle—from youth workers to teachers, from coaches to social workers—who have made decisions to go well beyond what could reasonably be expected of them in caring for a young person. Yet in almost every youth development role I've ever held, I've been told how important it is to maintain strong professional boundaries and avoid getting too involved with any individual young person. In theory, this makes sense. In practice, however, sometimes a young person needs more than we're *supposed* to give. The decisions we make in those moments shape not only the lives of the young people we care about but also our own. I call it **intervening when they need you most.**

This final Vital Connection may challenge what you've been taught about youth development and even some of your fundamental beliefs about where to draw professional boundaries. Over the years, it has certainly tested my own convictions and commitment about how to serve young people in need.

In the early 2000s, when I first began to research the role of caring adults and what made the biggest difference for young people, I was struck by a specific theme. When young people were interviewed about what had the biggest impact in their lives, they consistently pointed to people who had been there for them when no one else was. I read stories of young people who were bailed out of jail, offered housing when faced with homelessness, given a job when nobody else would hire them, and had their school fees paid. I was especially struck by the fact that all these examples seemed to go well beyond the limits of any youth development professional's prescribed role.

These stories were visceral, poignant, and powerful. They revealed examples of caring adults who went far beyond making time to hang out with or offering an additional daily dose of praise to a young person. These stories were about adults who took risks with their own careers and resources and remained involved even when it was difficult. They were adults who stepped into a messy situation and tried to make it better. These young people may have had other caring adults in their lives, but they remembered and deeply valued the person who showed up for them in ways that nobody else would or could.

Even though I first started reading these stories back in the early 2000s, it took me more than a decade to truly understand what it meant. As I've mentioned, I'm an activities guy by nature. The other Vital Connections are all tangible to me. I can picture exactly when and how I can apply these techniques to my work with young people. As a firm believer in equality, my aim has always been to try to ensure that each young person I work with gets an equal dose of each of these Vital Connections. Yet I came to realize, both from the research and examples I witnessed with my own eyes, that a caring adult willing to go beyond equal treatment and professional boundaries sometimes gave that young person what they really needed—and that action often made all the difference.

CROSSING MY OWN LINES

In 2008, I received an email from one of the staff members I worked with at CITW in Malawi. His name was Symon Chibaka. To his friends and colleagues, he was known as Moni. I'd worked closely with him for more than four years. In that time, he had risen from staff member to camp director. When he contacted me, he shared his aspiration to eventually manage the entire program. To do this, he felt he needed certain skills only a business certificate could provide. He could not afford the tuition, and he humbly asked for my assistance.

With little hesitation, I said yes. It sounded like it was going to be difficult to verify the actual full costs of the tuition. And it was unclear how to get the money to him securely. Despite these hurdles, however, I found myself emailing him almost immediately to figure out how we could make it work. Over the following few weeks, I reflected on the reasons why I was so quick to respond affirmatively. The answer shouldn't have surprised me. It was the exact reason the adults I read about in the research did what they did for the young people in their lives. The answer was love.

I loved Moni. He had become one of my favorite people to work with, anywhere in the world. I had already invested so much time with him in his development and in our friendship and I could see that he was poised to take his career and his livelihood to the next level. He was going to have a huge impact on his organization, and his next career steps would help him elevate his entire family to a new socioeconomic level. In addition, I knew he would be amazing at the job he aspired to, and I couldn't stand by and watch him stymied by the financial barrier of tuition. So I broke a set of rules I had followed for many years. I put much more of myself—financially and emotionally—into Moni than any professional rule book would call for. I did what needed to be done, not what I was supposed to do. I loved and believed in him, and when presented with the opportunity to do something to show how committed I was to him, I said yes.

There are times in all our lives when we desperately need a break. We need something to go our way or, at the very least, not to get any worse. This chapter is about the why and the how of adults who care so much that they are willing to do what's needed, even if their actions go against conventional approaches to supporting young people. It's a tribute to those who make that commitment. It's also a short guide to how you might go about emulating them if you find yourself in a similar situation.

In a sense, there's no way to design or practice this Vital Connection. Unlike the other five, it can't be broken down into easily digestible techniques or blocks of time. Unless you've formed a deep connection with a person, see them struggling, and know that you have it within your power to make a powerful difference, it's unlikely you'll even consider an intervention of this kind. However, for the sake of your own development as a caring adult, I hope you do face this type of scenario and have to wrestle with the question of whether to intervene. As Kailash Satyarthi, children's rights advocate and activist, echoing the words of Rabbi Hillel, said, "If not now, then when? If not you, then who?"

WHAT IS INTERVENING WHEN THEY NEED YOU MOST?

Intervening when young people need us the most blurs the lines between following the rules and doing what's needed. It also blurs the lines between treating young people equally and treating them fairly. Equality in working with groups of young people usually means that we divide up what we have evenly, giving each approximately the same portion. This could take the form of anything from distributing snacks—one banana per participant—to time and energy, to regularly praising each participant.

Equal treatment helps us avoid being accused of playing favorites. It can also help us manage fragile dynamics in a group or team. However, it doesn't address a crucial issue. The reality is that some young people have more critical needs than others. Giving each participant one banana works if we know that everyone ate lunch earlier in the day. However, what if we have a participant who hasn't had a full meal all day? Doling out praise to everyone, in small equal portions, may help keep the peace in a group, but what if one participant is chronically depleted, with an emotional tank near empty, because no one has said anything positive to them all week?

Sometimes young people need more than we are supposed to offer, no matter how much we bend our programs to meet their needs. This is an important reality to confront. We look at certain young people in our program, and in our hearts we know that no matter what we do, it probably won't be enough. Intervening when they need you most is a choice to step into a young person's life in a way that goes beyond your professional role. I cannot say that it's always the right decision. It's a difficult choice that may carry real risks. You may provoke disapproval from the young person's caregivers or your colleagues. Your intervention may not bring about the desired results, instead creating resentment and disappointment.

All I can advocate for is that we confront these circumstances more honestly, with an understanding of what is at stake when our programs and our own formal responsibilities aren't enough.

TYPES OF INTERVENTIONS

While it's impossible to cover all the different reasons you might want to intervene, there are three different scenarios that seem most common: the **launch scenario**, the **prevention scenario**, and the **rescue scenario**.

The **launch scenario** offers you, as a caring adult, the chance to pull a young person toward an experience or an opportunity that will most likely put them on a significantly better trajectory in some area of their life. Perhaps you know a young person who is trying everything they can to seek employment. They struggle in the interview process and are facing rejection after rejection. Yet you believe that if they could just get a job, they would excel at the work.

You may choose to intervene on their behalf with the owners of a local coffee shop, explaining that you're willing to vouch for the young person and support them as they adapt to the demands of a job. You ask them to give this young person a chance.

The **prevention scenario** involves your intervening to

avert a precarious or potentially damaging situation. For example, perhaps you know a young person who is at risk of expulsion from school for low grades and poor attendance. You may decide to drive them to school or sit with them after school to help them with their studies.

Foster parents operate in a long-term prevention scenario. Adoption can be an intensely traumatizing experience for a young person. It cuts at the core of attachment and a young person's needs for a stable and predictable caregiver. Even for children adopted at birth, or before they are old enough to remember their birth parent(s), adoption leaves its mark. The most skilled and successful foster parents understand that they are working with an inherently vulnerable young person, one who may have more basic needs than those of other young people their age and who may need additional support to mitigate some of the hurdles they encounter.

The **rescue scenario** occurs when you decide to step in to assist a young person already in a crisis, trying to stop a damaging or difficult situation from getting much worse. The grandmother I met on the train was rescuing her granddaughter.

Deciding whether to intervene in a young person's life can be a difficult moment. It tests our investment, our commitment, and even our sense of self. It tests our ethics and values. It challenges our own understanding of what we mean when we tell a young person we will be there for them, no matter what.

If you're thinking of intervening when a young person needs you most, you'll need to be ready to invest in him or her beyond the scope of a professional relationship. You may need to commit additional time, effort, money, and other resources. You may also need to prepare for potential criticism from your colleagues, who may question why you are singling out a certain young person for this kind of support.

Once you cross that line, you're inherently more involved. The relationship may become complicated. You may find yourself obliged to intervene further, because it's tough to intervene, but it's even tougher to step away once you've done so. This is not to deter you; it's simply a warning that there are ample reasons to intervene *and* not to intervene, each of which merits careful consideration.

PUTTING IT INTO PRACTICE: INTERVENING WHEN THEY NEED YOU MOST

As you may have realized, there's no cookie-cutter mold for practicing this Vital Connection. The way you choose to intervene will be determined by the need. Some young people affect us in ways that compel us to consider taking the kinds of actions described above. The form of your intervention will come from a deep understanding of the needs of the young person. When you know them so well that you understand that a type of intervention is critical, your actions will be guided by that knowledge. Interventions are complicated. Once you decide to step in, you will probably need to stay committed, lending your time, effort, and creativity to the task of helping the young person you have decided to support, for as long as they need you.

Before you decide to take this step, I invite you to consider four aspects of the situation. The first is the **best- and worst-case scenarios**. Ask yourself: What range of outcomes could your intervention lead to? Could it have unintended consequences? Have you thought it through carefully? Do you feel comfortable taking responsibility for any unforeseen problems that emerge due to your actions?

The second is the **potential impact**. What will be the cost to you and to the young person? Assess the time, effort, and financial and emotional cost of intervention. Take the time to look at the varied sides of this equation. Gauge the impact on the young person and take equal time to gauge the impact on you.

Third, before you step in, seek out **feedback and per-**

spective from one or more people in your network whom you trust. Triangulate your perspective and look for your blind spots. Unless the situation has already reached crisis point and demands immediate action, always take the time to consult other people.

Finally, I always recommend that you do a **gut check** before committing. Ask yourself: Why am I motivated to help this young person? Do I have the skill, will, and commitment to see the situation through? Have I thought this through? It's important to keep your eyes open, because you're contemplating a big step.

If your desire to act passes these four tests, then go ahead. This can be the harder path for you, but it's the path that provides a roof and a bed when there is none, an opportunity to stay in school in the face of expulsion, the chance to achieve a dream that seems unreachable, and even a way out when every other option seems closed.

The grandmother I met on the train did survive. She tracked me down a few years later and we spoke on the phone for a few minutes. Her health was good. Although her daughter was still struggling with her life in Florida, her granddaughter was doing well and enjoying life in Chicago. Moni completed his degree and, soon after, received the offer to become country director of the CITW program.

These are two success stories. Not all interventions turn out so well, but that doesn't mean it's not worth the risk.

CONCLUSION

LOVE REALLY IS THE ANSWER

* * * * * * *

Over the past two decades, I've had the pleasure of working with staff from hundreds of youth-serving organizations in close to twenty countries. In a significant number of these circumstances, the work could not have happened without a stellar interpreter. These interpreters often make all the difference in whether anything I say has resonance. I've learned that their language skill is only a piece of the equation. The best interpreters I've worked with immerse themselves in the content, eventually becoming extensions of the training team. As a result, they're able to discuss the training topics as if they created the training. Often, they internalize the content, applying it to their own lives.

In 2005, while delivering trainings on resilience in southern Thailand, I worked closely with two such people. For several weeks, we trained together all day, reviewing training materials in the evening, and sharing many meals together.

At dinner one night, one of our interpreters turned to me and gently inquired whether she could speak with me. She shared that the workshop material was making her think about many aspects of her own life, including her parenting. Her son was about seven or eight years of age at the time. She was very close to him, and it was clear that she loved him deeply. During the several weeks we were working together, she spoke to him on the phone at least once or twice a day. As we spoke, she leaned in a bit closer and said, "I have a story about my son. I think it's about resilience." This is what she shared with me.

Her son returned from school one day, visibly upset. She asked him about his day, and he said, "Something happened today in school and I want to tell you about it." She was nervous but determined to do everything she could to reassure him, so she encouraged him to share his experience.

He began, "Mom, before I tell you what happened, I have some questions. Is it true that before I was a boy, I was once a sperm?"

This was not the question she was expecting. Lost for words, she simply said, "Yes."

"Mom," he said, "is it also true that when I was a sperm, I was not the only sperm?"

Not knowing what else to say, she again said, "Yes."

"OK," he said, "I have one more question." By this time, she was close to panic.

"Mom, is it true that when I was a sperm, we had to swim?"

She was completely dumbfounded. All she could do was nod and, once again, say, "Yes." Seemingly satisfied with these answers, her son finally appeared ready to tell the rest of his story.

"Mom, something happened in school today. And I hope you won't be upset." With that, he began to cry. "We had gym class today, and there were relay races. I tried so hard, but I lost every single race."

Still confused, she tried to comfort him and tell him that it was OK.

Wiping away his tears, he said, "I know, Mom, but I just need you to know that once I was the strongest swimmer."

RESILIENCE IS FORGED THROUGH LOVE

To this day, I marvel that this boy, experiencing a harsh blow to his self-efficacy in gym class, somehow found strength and comfort in the fact that at conception, as a sperm, he once outswam several hundred million competitors to win that crucial race. If only each of us were that resilient and, if needed, could think that far back in our life story to gain strength and confidence. My hope is that more young people, when confronted with challenges, setbacks, or obstacles, will find that kind of self-efficacy to draw on.

For many young people, the world is a painfully unfair place, and too often we are unwilling or unable to listen to what they really need. Some are faced with obstacles that would crush many adults, let alone children or teenagers. This book is an attempt to give those young people a voice. They may not always have the words to explain what they need. In some cases, they may be telling us exactly what they need, only to go unheard due to our lack of skill or understanding. In other cases, their suffering may be so great that their needs—and words—are locked inside. What we know is that the power of relationship is remarkably protective. It serves as an incredible buffer, supporting us as we face adversity and vulnerability.

Bruce Perry, in *The Boy Who Was Raised as a Dog*, writes,

"Without love, children literally do not grow."[10] Love protects. Love nurtures. Love heals. My aspiration in this book has been twofold: first, to reveal the power of relationship to transform how you can work with young people; second, to share some of the best and most useful ways I know to tap into that power and have the greatest possible impact on their lives.

Intentional programming and curriculum matter. Safe facilities matter. Strong program culture matters. Vital Connections matter more. Resilience and self-efficacy are not attributes that we develop in isolation from other parts of our life. As humans, we have always found strength, protection, and support in other humans. Our connections with others are essential to our survival. We are born into this world unable to fend for ourselves. Without caring adults, we cannot survive.

A special power exists in the connections between adults and young people. The six Vital Connections described in this book have evolved from exploring the research about caring adults and witnessing firsthand, in the field, the many different ways that skilled youth workers utilize this power.

---

10 Bruce Perry and Maia Szalavitz, *The Boy Who Was Raised as a Dog, and Other Stories from a Child Psychiatrist's Notebook: What Traumatized Children Can Teach Us about Loss, Love, and Healing* (New York: Perseus, 2017).

Each Vital Connection corresponds to a distinct and fundamental need. Young people may not always be able to articulate their needs, but they exist nonetheless. If we know what to look for, we have an opportunity to meet those needs. Reem knew what to look for during Team Time in Gaza. Kwinji knew what to look for after soccer practice in Zimbabwe. Karn knew what to look for at bedtime in Thailand.

A tug on your arm, an invitation to play, lingering before or after a program—these are all subtle requests for your **time**. Sharing personal information, giving you insights into their lives, and talking about their interests or aspirations—these are all attempts to be seen, to become familiar to you, to be **known**.

Asking you, "How did I do?," sharing tales of success and failure, looking to you for approval and support—this is how young people learn that you **believe** in them. Seeking out your advice, sharing a challenge they are facing, or telling you a secret—these are ways of engaging you in **conversation**.

Telling you how they are doing in school, revealing some of their greatest struggles, sharing their hopes and dreams for the future—these should serve as reminders that you cannot be everything to a young person. They need **a bigger community**. These signals can also challenge you to reflect deeply on the question of your **commitment** and how you can provide what they may truly need, regardless of the expectations placed on someone in your role.

One of the most exciting things about Vital Connections is how portable they are and how often they can be applied in day-to-day interactions with young people. For the most part, they do not require planning. You do not need paper, pen, or any other equipment. You can use them in a classroom, a sports field, on a drive or a walk, over the dinner table, on the phone, in a text, or in any other setting where you are interacting or working with a young person.

Most importantly, they work. Vital Connections can work in an instant, when you offer an affirmation or a few seconds of praise. They work when you have a few minutes to listen to a young person's story or help them connect with another caring adult. They work when you need to sit down and have a long, in-depth conversation with a young person or figure out together how to handle a difficult situation.

Vital Connections are not intended to replace existing curriculum or activities that you use to have a positive impact on the lives of young people. They are additional tools, forming a crucial piece of a complicated youth development puzzle.

I believe our power to impact the lives of individual young

people is often much greater than we imagine. If you're unsure where to begin, start by thinking closely about what they need. Then listen a little longer, look a little more closely, and lead with love.

WATERING CANS

My work with the CITW camp in Malawi spanned the years between 2004 and 2008. During that time, I formed a strong bond with many of the local staff. I traveled there four times, each trip lasting at least a month. During those years, I witnessed a profound transformation in the staff. They grew from having little to no experience in youth work to becoming a tightly knit team of skilled camp counselors and leaders.

For the first few years, we struggled to name the camp. On the surface, it seemed like a task we could have checked off our to-do list with relative ease. However, it proved more challenging than I had first imagined. In the local languages, there simply wasn't a word for "camp" that didn't carry the connotations of a refugee camp. Additionally, we couldn't find the right term for "counselor" or "camper." There were words for "teacher," "coach," and "student," but none of them captured the special role played by a counselor, nor the unique identity associated with being a camper.

As I quickly discovered, there were multiple languages

in Malawi, from Chichewa to Yao to Chitumbuka. What worked in one language failed the translation test in another. For example, we had tried to use the name *Children of the Wilderness*. In some dialects, those words translated well, but in another, the same phrase translated to "Children from the Dirt." Understandably, this was considered highly offensive. Despite our best efforts in those first seasons of work, we never succeeded in settling on a good name for our camp.

This all changed on one of my later visits. A staff member approached me excitedly and declared, "I think I know what to call it!"

I was excited. "Tell me," I said.

"We can call our camp *Chigow n'di m'pozwa!*"

"What does that mean?" I asked.

"Little baby cassavas that need lots of water and care to grow."

In Malawi, cassavas are a staple food. They're also a very difficult crop to grow. They require great attention and careful watering. I smiled, my pulse quickened, and I felt a deep appreciation for what he was saying.

"So what does that make you—the staff?" I inquired.

Without skipping a beat, he exclaimed, "Oh, we're the watering cans!"

"Yes," I said. "That's perfect."

LET'S CONNECT

I believe that Vital Connections are superpowers we all possess. They are lying dormant, waiting for us to activate them. They do not require a fancy facility or complicated curriculum. They do not require intensive planning. Most of the time, they do not cost any money.

It is my hope that the techniques described in this book can enhance your existing youth development tool-kit. If you'd like to bulk order books for friends, family, colleagues, or anyone else, you can email me at info@ loubergholz.com. At Edgework, we facilitate a series of Vital Connections workshops. Attending a workshop is a special opportunity to learn and practice an even broader set of techniques than those contained within these pages. If you'd like to know more about bringing a Vital Connections workshop to your organization, please be in touch.

For every technique shared in this book, I'm certain many more exist that haven't been captured in these pages. Nearly every time I facilitate a workshop, a participant shares a special way that they make time at the right time or a unique method of supporting a vital conversation.

Now that you've read these Vital Connection stories, I'd love to read yours. Share your successes and struggles. Send along your best Vital Connection techniques. There are so many exceptionally skilled and dedicated youth workers around the world, and we can all benefit from your expertise. Maybe I'll have the privilege of sharing *your* story in a future edition of this book.

ACKNOWLEDGMENTS

* * * * * * *

My career has been shaped by the many people and organizations I have had the privilege of working with and learning from: from wise professors to brilliant youth workers and mentors, and thousands of children and adolescents, from Cleveland to Addis Ababa.

Some of the people listed here have been colleagues for years, even decades, while others were part of my life for a shorter time. Vital Connections can influence a life in any number of ways. So I express my deep gratitude to the people here in chronological order, to trace the origins and sequencing of the people and experiences that have shaped the writing of this book.

First, I want to thank my parents, Eleanor and David. In different ways, each influenced my orientation to working with young people and my understanding of how positive outcomes emerge through relationships. They supported this nontraditional career path I have been on since my early twenties and the many different contexts I've explored in service of this work. Eleanor, an accomplished journalist and author of two books, played an indispensable editorial role at crucial junctures in this process, and I am indebted to her for her expertise, insight, and the many hours she dedicated to helping me write this book. Thank you, Mom.

My initial work in youth development spanned numerous summer camps, Boys and Girls Clubs, preschool settings, a residential treatment center in the forest in New Mexico, and new immigrant absorption centers in Israel. However, my investment in the topic of this book began in earnest in 1998 when I began to work with the Hole in the Wall Gang Camp in Connecticut, a unique organization dedicated to working with children and families affected by life-threatening illnesses.

That summer, I ran their adventure program, which launched my work with both the organization and the broader association of camps, the SeriousFun Network. It was a partnership that eventually spanned more than fifteen years and a setting in which I saw the power of relationship in its purest form, not only as a buffer against life's hardships but also as a source of strength, health, and healing. I am indebted to many of the people I worked with as part of the SeriousFun Network, each of whom helped reveal to me special aspects of the power of Vital Connections. They are Karen Allen, Mwenya Kabwe, Padraig Barry, Alex Robertson, Jules Porter, Caroline Stott, Sarah Eio Smithson, Kevin Rice, James Canton, Nancy Campbell, Steve Nagler, and Aly Fox.

My work with the SeriousFun Network sent me to Namibia and Malawi between 2002 and 2008 to help develop two unique camp programs for an organization called Children in the Wilderness. Sunday Nelenge from Namibia and Symon Chibaka from Malawi are two of the most skilled youth workers I have ever known. It has been such a pleasure to work with and learn from them. I also want to thank Ben Forbes and Amanda Joynt, as well as the many staff I worked alongside in both countries. You bore the challenge of my relentless pushing for the "more" we could do for the children we were serving, along with the countless cheers, games, late-night meetings, and renditions of "Ketchy Ketchy."

At the tail end of my work on these camps in Africa, I was lucky enough to consult with the Worldwide Orphans Foundation in Ethiopia, piloting a camp project for a population of children between six and nine years old. I spent two summers working on bringing this camp to fruition, collaborating closely with Mimi Asfaw, Lemlem Tale, Selam Wagaw, and an awesome team of counselors and support staff.

I first met Bill Kubicek at the Hole in the Wall Gang Camp in 1998 and worked for him, starting in 1999, to build Next Step, an organization dedicated to helping young adults break through the limitations often associated with life-threatening illnesses. We spent ten years exploring many distinct ways in which relationships move and transform people, perfected epic late-night informal time, and saw firsthand the power of helping young people get connected to the right people at just the right time.

During this same period in the early 2000s, by a strange set of circumstances that merit their own chapter in a future book, I found myself in Bulawayo, Zimbabwe, taking up temporary residence in a beautiful compound. There, I typed furiously on my computer, accompanied by Kirk Friedrich, one of the three founders of Grassroot Soccer. I was in Bulawayo for approximately two weeks. By the end of that trip, we had created what would become the foundation curriculum for one of the first-ever sport-based HIV prevention programs in Africa. I worked on and off with Grassroot Soccer through 2010, and it was while working with Kirk, Jeff DeCelles, Tommy Clark, and many other incredible people in their organization that I began to understand how Vital Connections could be taught and embedded inside programs.

I met Martha Myers in Malawi around 2008. When she moved to the Middle East the following year, her remarkable vision helped bring to life the Eye to the Future project in Gaza that I would eventually work on between 2009 and 2013. Thanks to Martha, Yazdan El Amawi, Mona Jaber, Ahmed El Hinnawi, Sa'id, Madhoun, and the rest of the leadership staff from CARE International and Mercy Corps. Thanks also to our four incredible interpreters—Amal El Shanti, Amani Al Nawajha, Rudaina Abu Nada, and Hala Safadi—and to the 160-plus mentors with whom we worked. It was with Eye to the Future that I had the chance to create a full intervention for children built on the foundation of Vital Connections. Aided by the wisdom of Dr. Wendy D'Andrea and her team, who conducted our evaluation, we gathered key data that helped us make the case for the ways in which relationships can change the lives of children.

It was in Gaza, one of the most complicated places in the world, with chronic levels of toxic stress and intergenerational trauma, that I witnessed a group of staff internalize the Vital Connections skillset, applying it first to their own lives and families and then to the several thousand children the program was serving. They showed how powerful relationships can be in mitigating and healing the consequences of violence. I will never forget the moment in 2012 when more than a hundred staff from five different project sites gathered at the Lighthouse Restaurant on the Gazan coast and looked at the evaluation results together, and the buzz of joy and tears that passed through the group when we all saw the impact the program was having.

Although I love to read and synthesize data, I am not a traditional researcher. My skills lie in looking for themes, trends, and insights in the research that is being conducted by others. My work on Vital Connections owes a tremendous debt of gratitude to the many people and organizations who are conducting frontline studies and evaluations that are contributing to our understanding of the role of caring adults in the lives of young people. They include Bessel van der Kolk, Bonnie Benard, Bruce Perry, Carol Dweck, Joyfields Institute, Margaret Blaustein, Martha Bragin, Martin Seligman, Michael Brandwein, Michael Unger, Robert Brooks, Sam Goldstein, and the Search Institute.

Writing a book is not an easy undertaking. I am indebted to the team at Lioncrest Publishing for guiding me through the process and playing instrumental roles in the crafting of this book. I express my deepest gratitude to publishing manager Emily Gindlesparger, editor Rob Wolf Petersen, and outliner Holly Hudson.

Finally, I want to mention the wonderful colleagues and mentors who have had major influences on this body of work over the past twenty years, including Charlie and Wendy Harrington, Jonah Geller, Mike Brown, Tracey Britton, Maren Rojas, Amy Goldfarb, John McCarthy, Megan Bartlett, Megan Gildin, Meredith Whitley, Allison Task, Patti Papapietro, Andrea Parrot, and Judy Ross Bernstein.

Thank you to the entire "village" it took to bring this book to life.

ABOUT THE AUTHOR

• • • • • • •

 **LOU BERGHOLZ** is founder and managing partner of Edgework Consulting, a Boston-based firm that provides staff/leadership development and capacity building to organizations around the world. An important component of the company's work supports innovative approaches to youth development, particularly among under-resourced populations affected by trauma. Lou is a much sought-after keynote speaker, program designer, and facilitator who has worked on four continents. He has worked with a wide range of organizations and children's causes, including the SeriousFun Network, CARE International, UNICEF, Grassroot Soccer, Boys and Girls Club, Up2Us Sports, and the Justice Resource Institute.

73119007R00129

Made in the USA
San Bernardino, CA
01 April 2018